Who We Were

Life Since the Iverson Sod House

Stories by Victor Johnson

ISBN 978-1-938911-88-0

Library of Congress Control Number: 2017903170

Smith Printing
17343 Wolverine Street NW, Ramsey, MN 55303 • 1-800-416-9099 • www.SmithPrinting.net
Printed in the USA

Acknowledgements

I first must thank Michael Cotter and Beverly Jackson, who personally introduced storytelling to me when I came only to listen to others tell their stories at meetings of the Storytellers Guild in Austin, MN. They were my informal teachers who assured all who came, "Everyone has a story to tell". I soon found that it was safe to tell from my own memories. They had a simple acceptance that gave each of us self-confidence to tell "Our Story."

I appreciate that my adult children urged that my oral stories needed to be put on paper, so that we would be able to retain these previously unwritten heritage stories. At Christmas time in 2004, I rewarded each in the family with a photocopied booklet of my first unedited seven short story efforts. Since then, the idea of a bound book grew, when I realized that I was the only person alive, who would ever tell some of the happenings that begged to be retained in print.

What a joy to discover that each area in Norway has an archivist, retained by the government, to maintain historic records and stories of all the Norwegian families in their area, especially those who emigrated to America from 1834 to 1924. Their office retains genealogical records as far back as the years in 1600.

The archivists, Arne Inge Saebo in Balestrand and Rasmus Sunde in Vik, furnished facts and stories which were indispensable for the first chapter in this book.

I really appreciate the efforts of my new friend, Carol Dahl, for the report of her research revealing the time and place of the marriage of Ole and Brita Iverson and information about their voyage on the Juno.

As I began to assemble the chapters in this book, I had a strong feeling of sadness to think that the tales about the Schanke Dell Store might be lost forever, since my knowledge was incomplete of those many happenings that are lovely to tell. I appreciate the help of Beverly Teskey, who retrieved from the Faribault County Historical Society, a photocopy of speech notes written by LaVonne Volz who, at some time in the past, must have given a speech about facts that helped complete that chapter. Unfortunately Lavonne died in 2015; she and her family lived a short distance from the store and her notes provided what might be the last of those Dell tales not lost in time.

Had my friend, Duffy Erdahl, lived to tell me more, I would have had a more adequate supply of delightful tales about Valdy and Thoralf Schanke.

I sorely needed the efforts of our wonderful "roof-mate", Barbara Schue, who with her husband, John, live next door in our duplex and who claimed that she "just loves to edit books" for aspiring authors. Her efforts polished the sometimes awkward wording that results from transposing oral stories from the memory of an author, who talks "Minnesota Nice", and whose knowledge of spelling has always been inadequate.

I could never have found a better person to design the cover of the book than my wife's son-in-law, Don Mack, a professional internet web artist. That he found a picture of the side of a sod house baffles and delights me.

Neophite authors, like me, should always contact Becky Smith of Smith Printing in Anoka, MN to accomplish tasks that one cannot imagine can be done to polish the final book product. Becky accomplishes miracles.

Our utmost thanks must be extended to our distant relatives in Norway, distant on our family tree and distant because of an ocean between us: John Petter Roedal and his wife, Marit; Sigmund Roedal and his wife, Greta; and Bjorn Honsi and her husband, Jon Olav Afedt. Their gracious hosting of our various stays in their homes will always be remembered, especially because the visits to our relatives in Norway had been anticipated since I was yet a child.

Finally I thank God, that for these many years, He allowed me to observe, to tell, and to be a part of the stories about this place in this small community in Minnesota, USA.

Prologue

"They shall walk and not faint."

My earliest recollections of the happenings and memories from my very young life are of following closely behind and endlessly questioning the men who were the giants in my small world, as I absorbed their stories. They expanded my young imagination and instilled in me a desire to explore the places they had lived and to meet the people who lived there. These men were my father, Joseph Johnson, his Uncle Jens who lived with us, and Jens' brother, my grandfather, Ole Johnson. All of them treated me in a way which made me feel special, because they listened to my constant questions and responded as they would to an adult.

The most exotic place to me at the time was told about by Uncle Jens when he often began the story of his previous life in Norway with the words, *"Back in the old country"*. Those words made me stop and listen closely each time. I vowed to someday experience this place and meet the people that were part of our family.

It had to be done! In three trips to Norway in 1981, 1999, and 2007, our Norwegian relatives welcomed us with their special "red carpet treatment". On our first visit, John Petter Roedal took us to 43 different homes to meet all of our relatives that were in the area of Sykkylven, Norway.

View of Geirangerfjord *(Located near Sykklevan.)*

We experienced the two-room log home on the small farm half-way up the mountain above the village, where Grandpa Ole and Uncle Jens lived as children before they emigrated. In each successive trip we returned to Aasen (the farm name) to learn more each time. In 2007 we thrilled at the breath-taking panorama from the mountain top above Aasen which at one time had been the summer pasture for the local farmers' cattle, goats, and sheep. For the first time, limited vehicle traffic was able to drive to that pristine area, because of a recently formed rough rocky road.

During that first visit to Norway in 1981 our hosts, Sigmund and John Petter Roedal, treated us like royalty, but had no answers to my questions about my great-grandfather, Ole Iverson, who came to America 32 years before Ole Johnson's emigration. Where in Norway did Ole Iverson and his wife, Brita, live before they emigrated to America in 1856?

I only discovered that information, several years later, when I visited Leo Maland, who lived in Frost, MN. Leo had a copy of the original Emerald Church records of church events beginning in 1869, which were written in the Norwegian language. The Emerald Church was located about half-way between the Iverson farm and Frost, MN.

It was written on page 14 that my grandmother, Martha Iverson, was born on December 31, 1869 and was baptised on January 16, 1870. Her parents were Ole Iverson from 'Vigs Progj' and 'Britha' Nelsdatter from 'Balstrand Progj'. Now I knew.

I needed another trip to Norway in 1999 to discover more information about my great-grandparents, who were the first to come to this place on the prairie as homesteaders. On that trip, I discovered that many villages had a government employee called an "archivist", who had all the records and some stories of the emigration of 43,000 persons from Norway to America which transpired between 1839 and 1924. About twenty-five percent of all the youth in Norway left during that time in their desire to become "Americans".

I gathered a treasure trove of information and stories from the Vik archivist, Rasmus Sunde. He told that Ole Iverson lived, not on a farm, but in the village of Vig (often also referred to as Vik). Before marriage, Ole's mother came from a farm near Vik located near the Hopperstad Stave Church. When I visited the farm, I learned that perhaps I am descended from **Viking Royalty**. The story is written here and has been fun to tell.

As I prepared to assemble these stories, I realized that I was following my early desire for knowledge and exploration that was instilled in me so many years before as a young child.

My first response to recording my Norwegian family story was to try to use the field of genealogy, which had become a favored hobby of some of my friends and relatives. I soon realized that simply recording the history of the lineage succession, and the important dates associated, omitted the interesting life stories of the persons listed, which begged to be told and recorded. Everyone loves a story, even the littlest children at bedtime.

For a number of years, I belonged to the Storytellers Guild at Austin and Albert Lea, where the motto of the group was, *"Everyone has a story to tell."* It was there that I first realized that I had family stories that other persons seemed interested to hear.

Like a copy of the Reader's Digest, each of the chapters that are written here are individual stories which have touched my life in some way. These true stories describe the places and expose the unique personalities and activities of individuals, as I remember them. The time span of these stories cover four generations before me, and at this late date in my life there are already living, three generations that follow me, whose stories I shall leave for them to tell.

It was at age 81 that I first realized that my body was not keeping up with the opinion I had of my own physical abilities. We had habitually taken an annual family vacation by visiting my cousin, LaVern Hamre, who lived west of Denver in a mountain home that was seven switchbacks above Interstate 70. LaVern loved down-hill skiing and so did our family, so we continued this annual skiing activity with him, even after our children had left the nest.

On the last year that I skied at age 81, I could not understand why I did not have enough stamina to enjoy fighting gravity on the mountain slopes. I thought something serious might have happened to my body. My physician, with blunt honesty, advised that perhaps it was due to OLD AGE, which up to that moment I had chosen to ignore. I chose still to reject his conclusion.

My son, Matthew, rubbed it in when he instructed *"Dad, take your driver's license out of your pocket and look at the birthdate printed there."* I am forced to personally accept what my body, the doctor and my son were telling me—telling gently at first and then increasing in volume to gain my attention.

In 2011 at age 83, I was told that the pads between the lower vertebrae in my back had shrunk, causing me to be more than an inch shorter than I was as a younger man. My back ached and the pain extended to my ankle. I could no longer walk without pain and I could not stand up straight. After an MRI, surgeons found and removed a cyst which had pressured a nerve on my spinal column causing that problem. Relieved, I could walk upright without being bent over. However, I was told that my periodic back discomfort, due to the lack of spacing between my lower vertebrae, would continue. To my everlasting dismay, the doctor and my son had correctly diagnosed AGE to be the cause of my chronic condition.

I said, *"God, now I hear you. I realize I must no longer pretend I am still age 60."*

So I accepted that although I was in quite good health, I needed to leave our farm home, because I was unable to do many of the regular duties that were required by our living there.

I visited the realtor and listed our farmstead home that was a portion of the acreage where my Norwegian great-grandfather, Ole Iverson, had built and first lived in a sod house to meet the title requirements of the Homestead Law.

This was the first time that any part of that original homestead acreage would be sold to a family which was not part of our family lineage. I was of the fourth generation who had lived, loved and toiled on that property and had continued the unbroken family lineage of those who tilled and harvested on that parcel of formerly unbroken prairie sod.

A few years previous, shortly after the death of my wife, Irene, whom we called Rene, I attended a pot-luck luncheon with some of the members of the Storytellers Guild at the lakeside home of Beverly Jackson in Albert Lea, MN. We sat together on the deck overlooking the lake on that sunny summer afternoon with light-hearted conversation bouncing back and forth gleefully. With a big smile on her face, one of the ladies asked this question, *"Vic, now that you're single, have you thought of acquiring another wife?"*

I didn't hesitate, but in an attempt to dodge that quite personal question, I gave an answer that yet puzzles me as to its source and I responded totally in jest, *"Oh yes, I have decided to follow that old Yiddish rule that I shall find a wife that is half my age plus seven years."*

A short period of time elapsed, as the lady who asked the question pondered her mathematics and my estimated age before she replied, *"Oh Vic, you can't do that. You would never want to go through menopause again."* I'm still laughing at her advice, which I actually followed, and have now enjoyed eleven years with my wife, Eleanor Lindeman, who is much closer to my age than my Yiddish rule would allow.

It was at our wedding reception that a long-time friend, Marne Aleckson Blatchford, in a few words fully explained the life I was about to experience in my second marriage. Marne always displayed a lovely effervescent spirit that could never be contained as her love of life spilled out to infect everyone that was in her presence. She took my hand in her two hands to congratulate me as she quite emphatically exclaimed, *"Oh Vic, I'm so very happy for you. No one, but one who has lost their first loving spouse, can ever understand the special joy that happens when one takes a second spouse."*

Victor Johnson and Eleanor Lindeman.

Marne had experienced that joy and couldn't contain her exuberance. Her own children had introduced her to her second husband and she correctly predicted our "special joy" on that first day of our new marriage. For eleven years now, Ellie and I have found and experienced that joy that Marne aptly described.

When my parents chose to retire from the farmstead on which they had toiled all their married life, they desired to buy a home in Blue Earth, MN. I knew of and suggested a nice home that was available on a quiet cul-de-sac, which I thought they might like. As the owners were about to show their home to my parents, my outspoken mother blurted as soon as she stepped into the first room, "*This is my house. I want it*". The price negotiations became complete at that moment. The second home of their life time was located on this quiet cul-de-sac with neighbors of like kind and of similar station in life.

Freda Gunderson, a widow of Norwegian descent who lived across the street, was the lovely "house mother" of the community. She would often invite the closest neighbors for morning coffee and kringla at her home. One of the widows occasionally had not completely prepared herself for the day, yet without delay she would "pad" across the street in her slippers and housecoat.

My parents found an earned solace in their retirement with loving, accepting neighbors, who together shared of themselves in that comfortable community. Now when I write their story, I realize I too have found that same special earned solace.

We moved to "Timber Hills" which is a lovely campus for those of our age. We acquired a three-bedroom townhouse located on Burnham Circle which is a street with 67 townhouses located on each side of the circular street which are all occupied by persons of similar age and station in life. Like my parents in their Blue Earth cul-de-sac of retired persons of similar age and station in life, we also have neighbors whom we enjoy and with whom we share numerous activities. Although, unlike Freda Gunderson in my parents' retirement cul-de-sac, we have found no one who bakes and serves kringla, but we have gracious neighbors who make life interesting and enjoyable as we do so many activities together.

As I aged, I realized that perhaps my past-told collection of family stories of things that really happened needed to be preserved or they would be forever lost, because they described a flavor of the past that only I could tell and perhaps some could not imagine.

Originally it had been at the urging of my family that I first reduced these stories to print, which until then had remained only in my memory. Some of the stories are silly, some are sober, some are historic, some are so sad that in order to escape the pain, I choose to put them on a high shelf, almost too high to reach. By printing them now, I hope to preserve a small part of the history of our family that has extended over three centuries.

The chapters in this book are not intended to be consecutive, but rather are a compilation of stories formerly only told from memory, and now finally reduced to printed words. The stories range from the ridiculous to the sublime.

When I wrote the eulogy for Rene's funeral I referred to God's promises written by Isaiah in the Old Testament. As I reflected again on the eulogy and all of those in my heritage of whom I have written, I again ponder the meaning of those poetic biblical words where Isaiah wrote his story that told of the constant presence of God's grace in our lives and predicted:

They shall mount up on wings like eagles,
they shall walk and not faint.

Table of Contents

Chapter One

The Homestead

He has been death's guest,
He has sailed upon the thunder;
He has been christened wth fear
who has sailed the Sognefjord
from Fortun to Sygnefest.
Henik Wergeland (1808-1845)

Per Ivarson Undi and his wife Anna Davidsdotter and their two children were the first immigrants to leave Vik, Norway in 1839 and come to the United States. They settled in Wiota, Wisconsin. Later, Per wrote a letter to his brother in Vik, which was circulated and read by nearly everyone in that small community. This is what he wrote:

All who have come to America from Vik were doing very well and live like rich people. When you come, bring along with you a copper kettle, a griddle for making flatbread, and a rake auger. Bring your large broadaxe along if it is an excellent one; also a small axe, two hoes or three, if you have them, or sickles and sheath knives.

Ole Iverson was just 12 years old when he heard these words and he immediately was determined to come to America just like Per Ivarson Undi. It would be exciting to go to this unknown world. In his imagination he knew that he too could "do very well and live like rich people."

That next spring, with Per Ivarson Undi's words still ringing in his ears though he was only 12 years old, he traveled a long distance from the village of Vik to work on a fishing vessel in northern Norway for 9 seasons earning money to pay his fare to cross the Atlantic Ocean. Ole was determined to go to that exciting place Per Undi had described.

Vik is a small village on the south shore of Sognefjord. The fjord joins the ocean just north of Bergen and from there it intrudes almost to the center of the country. It is a deep fjord made up of a mix of fresh and sea water which is wide enough for ocean-going vessels to ply. It is approximately 3 or 4 miles wide in the area of the village of Vik. The Balestrand village is a bit further upstream on the opposite side of the fjord and about 10 miles from Vik.

At that time it cost about 50 specie dollars for an adult to travel from Bergen to America with reduced rates for children. A specie dollar had a value of about one American dollar at the time. (Norway used specie dollars until 1873, at which time it switched to the kroner.) Not everyone in Vik could afford to go to America. A farm laborer in Norway at that time would normally earn about 15 specie dollars in a year. For eight or nine years from age 12 to age 21, Ole may have earned a bit more each year by working instead on a fishing boat.

Ole was born in 1835. His mother's name was Guro Oldsdotter Honsi. His father was known as Skaffar-Ivar. He was called 'Skaffar' because of his occupation of hauling goods and people from town to town up and down Sognefjord with his 60-70 foot, single-masted freight boat. Perhaps his occupation might be compared to our over-the-road haulers with their 18-wheeler trucks.

The Iversons lived not on a farm, but in the village of Vik not far from the fjord. Although Skaffar-Ivar's vessel was fine for plying Sognefjord, it was small compared to the sailing ship with its three masts that would eventually take Ole and his younger brother, John, to Quebec, Canada.

Guro and Skaffar-Ivar had nine children born as follows: Brita 1827, Marta 1829, Peder 1831 Ole 1835, Hansine 1837, Synneva 1840, Anna 1843, John 1845 and Johannes 1847.

Finally at age 21 Ole had saved enough money to come to America. Ole's parents had saved enough money so that his younger brother, John, could travel to America with Ole. *John was only eleven years old when he left home.* *

It was the day his sons would be taken by Skaffar-Ivar in his sailing vessel to Bergen for the voyage across the Atlantic Ocean. Only the father and the two boys would make the trip down Sognefjord to Bergen, because Guro needed to attend to their four younger children who yet remained at home. As Guro walked down to the fjord with her two sons holding her hands, one on each side, she knew this would likely be the last time she would ever see these two sons again. Yet she was especially concerned about her son, John, because he was so very young to leave his mother and their home. She expected he might be homesick, so she prepared a special gift of a bag of nuts to pacify him if he became homesick. She hoped this luxury would help alleviate any homesickness.

Guro bid each of them goodbye and waved at Skaffar-Ivar who was already on board his vessel. When she had walked only a short distance toward her home, she turned for a final look to her family members as the vessel pulled away from the pier. What she saw put a smile on her tear-stained cheeks. Young John with his strong agile hands and legs had climbed to the very top of the single tall sailing mast of the freight boat. Holding on with one hand and two legs, with his other hand he was frantically waving final goodbye as he was about to leave forever his secure home in the village of Vik. He was sailing off to an exciting venture to America!

See Addendum 1.

It is known that the immigrants who sailed to America in those days could not travel light on the long trek to America. Each passenger had to guarantee to **bring a three-month supply of food** for themselves during the trip, which could last that long depending on the winds. We don't know exactly what Ole and John brought, but based on records of other travelers at the time, this perhaps might be the list of necessary supplies needed by two persons on this voyage:

5 cured mutton legs	1 barrel water
3 hams	coffee
42 pounds of butter	sugar
54 pieces of flatbread	syrup
2 ½ bushels potatoes	8 homespun underpants
2/3 bushel peas	8 homespun undershirts
150 pounds hardtack	8 sackcloth shirts
2/3 bushel home ground	18 pair woolen socks
rye flour	2 woven tapestries
1 barrel home-brewed beer	3 wool blankets

The tapestries and blankets were needed while on board ship as bedding. The wise immigrants often had trunks with a curved top to prevent the stacking of other trunks, thus allowing their regular access for daily needs.

There is a reported story about one woman from Arnafjorden near Vik whose ship was caught in a storm during the crossing. The captain wanted to throw all loose objects overboard, including her copper kettle. But the woman laid herself across the kettle, which was filled with flat bread, and said that if they were going to heave her copper kettle and her food overboard, well, then they could heave her overboard, too. The sailing voyage across the Atlantic was sometimes a test of endurance for the immigrants.

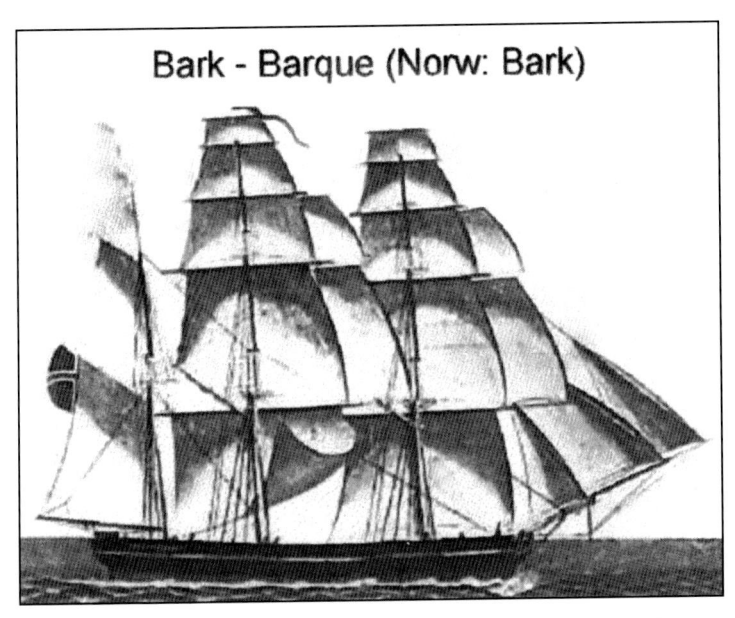

Bark - Barque (Norw: Bark)

The reason why this ship is called a bark is the way it's rigged.
It has three masts, with the foremast and mainmast square rigged and
the mizzenmast fore-and-aft rigged. A "bark" rigged vessel
could sail with fewer crew members.

The Bark or 'Barque' class of ships like the *Juno*, which had three masts, was faster than some other types of vessels at the time. The *Juno* often made the sailing voyage across the Atlantic to New York or Quebec in about 65 to 70 days. Actually the *Juno* once made the trip in 38 days.

This time the *Juno* left Bergen on April 30, 1856 and arrived in Quebec on July 5, 1856, taking 67 days for Ole and John to cross the ocean.

Ole's relative, Guttorm Tistel*, had immigrated much earlier than Ole and John and had traveled with his family to New York instead of Quebec. He had written to give advice to other immigrants from Vik. He advised to bring a minimum portion of their own water for each day of the trip since he was furnished only two small

*See his letter in Addendum 2.

glasses of water each day and felt he was dying from thirst. The water on his trip was not good water. He told that it smelled and tasted so terrible that he had to throw it up again.

Upon Guttorm's arrival in New York, a steam ship took them up the Hudson River to Albany. Then they traveled west by canal barge through the Erie Canal to Buffalo. This canal connected the Hudson River to the Great Lakes. The canal boats were drawn by horses that pulled from a path along the shore. The canal trip took from 12 to 15 days to get to the Great Lakes.

The boats were overfilled with standing room only. It was virtually impossible to sleep. In his letter he told of his tragedy while on the canal boat. Both his wife and his daughter, Thorbjorg, took ill and died before he got to Chicago. His wife was buried along the way, but he brought Thorbjorg's body with him to bury her in southern Wisconsin.

It was customary at that time for Norwegian friends or relatives to meet the new immigrants in Chicago and accompany them to settle in various locations in southern Wisconsin. Since the two young Iversons had relatives from Vik who had previously immigrated, it is safe to assume that they received a pleasant welcome upon arrival in Chicago.

Wisconsin records indicate that Ole Iverson married Brita Maeland on November 10, 1859 in Columbia County, Wisconsin. Brita had immigrated with her father on the same *Juno* voyage with Ole and John Iverson. My curiosity wonders whether they knew each other when they lived in Norway only 10 miles from each other. Archivists in Vik suspected that they were in love before the trip. The 1860 Wisconsin census revealed that they lived in or near the village of Vermont, in Dane County, Wisconsin, before they left to come to Minnesota in 1861. Dane County and Columbia County are adjacent to each other.

From the facts known, I suspect that Ole worked as a farm hand from the time he arrived in July, 1856 until sometime after the census was taken in 1860. He must have earned and saved enough to buy a team of horses, a wagon, necessary tools, perhaps a plow and enough provisions to help them cross the prairie and settle somewhere in Minnesota. Ole knew that if he would stake a claim to a large (in his estimation) acreage, improve it and live on it for 5 years, he would own free and clear a parcel of prairie land capable of growing beautiful crops.

His next effort would be to travel this great distance to an unknown place in Minnesota. Then he could accomplish what Per Ivarson Undi in his letter described when he told that *"Everyone from Vik were doing very well and live like rich people."* Ole and his recent bride, Brita, were off for a long trip behind two horses to the place of their dreams somewhere in Minnesota.

There were few places to cross the Mississippi River in 1860. I suspect they crossed the Mississippi River at Prairie du Chien, Wisconsin on the new steam-powered ferry. The horse-powered ferry had been replaced just a few years earlier in 1856.

Unknown immigrants traveling in 1865.

Arriving in Faribault County, Minnesota, Ole needed a nice location with good soil near a river for water to be available. He set stakes to determine the boundaries of 120 acres in Section 9 of Faribault County for his legal homestead. Next, he selected the location (about half-way between the eventual locations of the Iverson building site and the Johnson building site) for their sod house along the north side of the dirt road which crossed Ole's chosen homestead parcel. There, the dirt road actually had long been located a short distance north of the south border of his parcel, since the early Indians and travelers wisely went around the low land subject to flooding on the south edge of Ole's homestead.

He first removed the sod leaving a shallow hole the size of the home he was about to build. He cut many more sod 'bricks' from nearby untilled soil. The roots were tightly bound and held the soil together so that Ole and Brita could make sod bricks and pile them nicely around the shallow hole they had dug. After laying the sod bricks to make the walls, somehow they made a frame to hold the sod roof. In Norway many, if not most, of the homes in rural Norway had sod roofs, so Ole had knowledge from Vik about building a sod roof.

I know not how long Ole and Brita lived in their sod house, but I do know that they erected a log house as soon as they were able.

Being a new immigrant pioneer family was to experience many hardships including sickness and death. Ole and Brita (who usually used the English derivation, "Britha", sometime after immigration) had 11 children, but only 6 of them lived. They are as follows:

- Julia (Guro) Iverson Erickson (husband Arnt) born March 16, 1862
- Anna Iverson Ellingson (husband Arne) born March 8, 1864

- Synva (Sylvia or Susan) Iverson Anderson (husband John) born 1866
- Emil (Emmanuel) Iverson (wife Mary Birsack of Wells, MN) born August 31, 1868
- (Nels lived 1 day, born 1869)
- Martha Iverson Johnson (husband Ole) born December 31, 1869 (3 children were born and died young between 1869 and 1874)
- Bertha Iverson Chapman (husband Harry) born March 4, 1874.

Early picture of Iverson "Frame House".

The dates are unknown of the building of Ole and Britha's log cabin and later their frame house, that still remains and was our home when I was young. This house was moved in the early 1930's to make room for the widening of Highway 16. Prior to that time the road was known as Number 9 and the white house was very near to the road with the red barn also quite near and across on the south side of the road.

The Iverson "Frame House" in 2011.

Ole Iverson died in 1893. His brief obituary reads as follows:

"IVERSON – At his home in Emerald Township about 8 miles east of this city, Tuesday evening March 28, 1893 of Bright's disease Mr. Ole Iverson, age 58 years old and 3 days. Mr. Iverson settled in Emerald Township about 31 years ago, and by his well-known industry and strict integrity, had not only become one of the leading farmers, but a prominent citizen socially and politically. He had lived to see the sparsely settled country in which he settled nearly a third of a century ago developed into one of the richest agricultural sections in the west. He has been a victim for some time of the dread disease, and for some months has been a great sufferer. He leaves a wife and six children to mourn his death. The funeral will occur Saturday April first at 1:00 at the Lutheran Church in Emerald, near the residence of Ole Iverson. All friends of the family are invited."

[From Blue Earth City Post, March 30, 1893]

After Ole Iverson's death, Britha became the sole owner of their farm that had some farm buildings and a white two-story home with three bedrooms. She had no other place to reside. She was personally unable to operate the farm and had no ability to provide for herself, except whatever could be produced from the land.

This was at a time before automobiles and tractors. It was a time when horses were essential for transportation and for tilling the land. Any farm renter required the farm land and the barn to operate a farm and also needed a house for his family.

After Ole's death, Britha allowed the rental of her land for sixteen years previous to the date of the lease below, but the terms of those agreements are unknown. This lease is the only document remaining that tells the story of her survival after her husband's death. It has provisions that in today's agricultural commerce would indeed seem unusual.

In a delicate hand-written script on March 16, 1909, Britha Iverson agreed to a unique farm rental contract that actually provided the necessities of shelter and food for her most basic needs. Her creative life-saving lease, now framed, hangs on the wall above my desk.

Upon examining the penmanship, I conclude that the document likely was written by Iver Hedland, the tenant, and signed by Britha Iverson (signed as "Britha" on lease) as land-owner. The rent contract provided as follows:

[First party is Iver Hedland— Second party is Britha Iverson]

"Contract dated March 16, 1909
Contract ending March 1, 1910

(Contract begins on page 12)

Second party is to furnish five sheep and she shall furnish pasture for them on the farm on the north side and first party is to furnish hay for them. Each party shall have half of the increase and half of wool. Second party is to furnish all seed necessary to sow and plant said land except corn which first party is to furnish and potatoes and each party is to pay one half of the threshing machine bill for threshing the grain. After harvesting the crops to plow immediately before November 1st to with [sic] fifty two acres first party to haul out and spread on said premises before threshing all manure made thereon. First party to deliver on said farm the one half of all grains divided at the machine so raised and secured upon said farm said season and one half of all hay divided in the barn and in the stacks and two thirds of all corn divided husked in the corn crib on the premises. All the land in Section 16 shall be taken by the first party for a cash sum of $35 on October 1,1909 and a lien in favor of second party of all first partys share of crop corn and hay is hereby given to secure payment of said sum. Garden spot to first party free. Second party to have one third of potatoes divided in the cellar.

Second party reserves right to go unto the premises in fall of 1909 after harvest to prepare ground for a succeeding crop. Second party reserves the two east rooms downstairs and the southwest room upstairs and half of the kitchen and the right to live on the premises and reasonable use of that part thereof not used by first. Second party shall furnish first party one cow and he shall furnish second party milk cream and butter for her own use. The cow so furnished shall be delivered at end of this time, first party is to have increase. First party shall cut wood and prepare it for stove for second party near house and is to have his own stove wood free.

Iver Hedland first party
Britha Iverson second party"

As a young lad I was always fascinated by the several log houses that still remained standing in the neighborhood at the time. So I asked my father what had happened to the Iverson log house. After he advised me of its location, which was a grass spot between our barn and the machine shed, he told me the sad tale. Apparently it was still a standing structure when my father was a young lad. He said that in the later years of his youth they used it as a smokehouse to cure their hams, bacon and home-made sausages. It was his job to tend the fire and put sawdust on the glowing wood coals to produce the smoke. My father sheepishly admitted that it was his neglect that prevented me from ever viewing the Iverson log home. Because of his neglect, the fire got out of hand causing the log cabin to be completely destroyed by the fire. He never admitted to me what his discipline amounted to, but I suspect it was serious since the family not only lost the log cabin, but think about the hams, bacon, and sausages that were destroyed as well.

At that time Britha's daughter, Martha, and her husband, Ole Johnson, (my grandparents) lived close by, less than one quarter mile northwest of the original farmstead. A pasture and a grove of trees separated the two building sites.

The Johnsons had five children who now were Britha's to enjoy and to love. Often in the evening Ole and Martha would invite Britha to come to have the evening meal with them and their children. Britha loved those times at the end of her day that she could spend time with her grandchildren. After the meal, it would often be dark outside, so Ole or Martha would delegate one of their children to walk with Grandma Britha to her home through the pasture and the grove of trees. My father (Joseph Johnson) would always volunteer for this task, since he loved to be with his grandmother alone on those nighttime strolls through the pasture. He had another ulterior practical motive to be with her on the walk after the evening meal. After all, he had two sisters who could wash the dishes.

My father told me about a time that he walked with his Grandmother to her home in the dark that he never forgot. It happened in 1905 when he was ten years old. Their walk through the pasture took place at a time that was less than a year after the Wright Brothers made the first airplane flight in history in their makeshift airplane that flew 120 feet and was airborne for twelve seconds.

It was a dark evening. The moon had not yet come above the horizon. There was not a cloud in the sky. The stars were standing out in brilliant display. This awed my father since it seemed that there were more stars this night than he had ever seen before.
He said, *"Grandma, I wonder how many stars there are in the sky."*

Grandma Britha then prophesied as follows, *"The 'good book' says that the stars in the sky, like the hairs on your head, are so many that it is impossible to count them."* Then she went on, *"And the 'good book' says that man will go under the ocean and man will fly in the sky and it will be so thick that it will cover the sun."*

Perhaps there is only one time in history, past, present or future, that the prophesy of covering the sun with airplanes would come true. During World War II two hundred and twenty-five airplanes would leave England together to fly in formation to bomb Berlin. I imagine that would have been an impressive sight and would be capable of *"covering the sun"* as they continued through the sky on their mission.

My father told me that he had read that 'good book' from cover to cover and had never found that passage. I, too, have read that 'good book' from cover to cover and I did not find that passage either.

But as I imagine my father and his grandmother walking hand in hand through the pasture in the darkness of the night, I really believe a truth that we all know and believe---THAT GOD GIVES GRANDMOTHERS A VERY SPECIAL WISDOM.

Factual story compiled from oft-told handed-down tales as well as family documents. Other detailed facts obtained from the archivist's offices in Vik and Balestrand, Norway and detailed writings by archivists Rasmus Sunde and Arne Inge Saebo.

Chapter Two

You May Call Me
"Your Excellency"

In my quest to discover the Norwegian history of Ole and Britha Iverson, I found a treasure trove of information from the Vik archivist, Rasmus Sunde. Many villages have a government employee, called archivist, who keeps the historical records of the locality, including a detailed list of all who emigrated to America. These historical records included interesting stories about the farms and village homes and the way of life in Vik in the time of the 1800's. The Iverson ancestry can be traced back to 1600 A.D. in the records of the village of Vik.

My great-grandmother, Britha Iverson, came from the farm, Maeland, which was about ten miles and across the Sognefjord from Vik, and several miles north of Balestrand.

On our visit to Maeland, the farmer was just returning from the field with his empty "honey wagon", having just distributed liquid manure on his fields. He was happy to tell us the history of the farm, but warned us that he was NOT a relative of ours, because the family ownership of the Maeland farm had changed TWICE SINCE 1800.

It is apparent that in Norway, it is quite unusual for families to pass title outside of the family lineage. He brought out books and pictures, which we studied using the trunk of our rental car as a table to support the papers. In Norwegian culture the history of each farm is cherished and special.

The cultural stability of the farm history through generations is demonstrated by all persons who live on a farm traditionally taking their surname from the name of the farm, rather than the usual family lineage surname. This tradition often frustrates the tracing of family genealogies, particularly in the rare instance of a new owner purchasing the farm, in which case the family surname would change upon the new owner taking residence on the farm.

Vikoren is the earlier more formal name of the village, Vik or Vig. Apparently during previous times all families in the village assumed the surname, Vikoren, in a similar manner as persons who live on a farm assumed the farm name.

According to the records, nearly every home in Vik in 1875 had a small pen in their back yard, where they kept a pig, to be fed table scraps and other livestock feed during the year, to provide a handy 'garbage disposal' for the family. It was common to butcher the pig in preparation for the Christmas meals and as a supply of food during the winter months.

Rasmus Sunde told that the Iversons lived, not on a farm, but in the village of Vik on Sognefjord. Ole's father was a 'Skaffar' (boat-owner) and was known as "Skaffar-Ivar", just as his father before him, Hans Ivarson Vikoren was "Skaffar-Hans; their job was to provide transportation-for-hire for persons and supplies using a sailing vessel up and down Sognefjjord.

The Iverson home was a two-story house and was perhaps the largest house in Vik in 1875. In addition to his house, Skaffar-Ivar had a boat house and a small barn. At that time he had one cow, two sheep and the usual pig. He leased a plot to grow potatoes that was 1000 square meters in size. Rasmus Sunde concluded that according to these records, Skaffar-Ivar must have been considered a "rich man" at that time in Vik, Norway.

Ole Iverson's mother, Guri Olsdaughter Honsi, was born and raised on the farm, Honsi, which is near the ancient Hoppestad stave church, not far from the archivist office in Vik. There now remain only 28 stave churches in Norway, although originally there were over 1000. Of all the remaining stave churches, the Hoppers-tad stave church is the oldest, having been erected in 1130 A.D.

Bjorg Honsi Aafedt is a direct descendant of Ole Iverson's mother, who inherited Honsi when her father died. She told us that prior to 1936 the Norwegian law provided that the oldest SON shall inherit a farm upon the death of the owner. The law was changed in 1936 to provide that the oldest CHILD shall inherit the farm upon the death of the owner. She proudly told us that because she was born in 1935 and was the oldest child, SHE became a farmer and now owns Honsi.

Her father was still living when Bjorg married Jon Olav Aafedt who was a carpenter by trade. At the time of the marriage, Honsi needed a machine shed to house the farm machinery and Jon and Bjorg needed a home of their own.

Jon built a lovely two-story building on the south side of the Honsi farmstead. The lower level of the building opened to the north (toward Sognefjord) and housed the machinery. The upper level provided a lovely four bedroom apartment for Jon and Bjorg and their two children. They lived in the apartment until Bjorg's father died. After the death, Bjorg's mother, who was 25 years younger than her husband, moved into the apartment and the Aafeldt family moved into the "big house" on the farm.

Bjorg's mother eventually got employment in Oslo. She only uses the lovely apartment on her "holiday time" vacations, when she travels back to Honsi to be with the family. Bjorg welcomed us to enjoy the apartment during our time in the Vik and Balestrand area.

The window view of the fjord and the mountains beyond was magnificent. We were told that the apartment would be available whenever we should come to Norway, unless Bjorg's mother happened to be occupying it, which is seldom. Their hospitality was wonderful and we were invited for meals in the "big house" with the Aafedt family.

The small acreage of the farm was used for pasture for the dairy herd. On the walking tour of the farm with Bjorg and her two children, we first were shown the modern dairy barn west of the house. Then we hiked across the pasture toward the Hopperstad stave church which was on the opposite side of the road that bordered the west side of the pasture.

According to the opinion of those in the archivist's office, it is assumed that Ole Iverson was baptised in the Hopperstad stave church, based upon his birthdate in 1835.

The Hopperstad Stave Church. (Erected in 1130.)

In the pasture near the road was a mound of soil, perhaps 25-30 feet in diameter and maybe 4-5 feet deep with brush and other vegetation growing on the mound. Bjorg announced that this is where a Viking king was buried. When we returned back to the farmstead, I noticed a similar mound of soil half-way between the barn and the machine shed/apartment building. I queried Bjorg about this mound and was told that a Viking queen was buried there.

Moahaugan Viking Royalty Burial Mounds on Honsi Farm. (Circa 300-500 A.D.)

The next morning at breakfast, having contemplated the two Viking burial mounds located on the Honsi farm after returning from the farm tour the previous day, I wondered if there was more information about this Viking king and queen buried on the Honsi farm. I asked Bjorg a question that I had been thinking about. *"If there is a Viking King buried in the pasture near the Hopperstad Stave Church and a Viking Queen is buried here in your farm yard, are we related to Viking royalty?"*

Her answer remains indelible in my mind. Bjorg answered, *"We wondered that too. My cousin went to Oslo to study the records of Viking royalty. He said that we could be related to royalty, IF the Viking king sired a child when he was 100 years old."*

That's when I applied my own reasoning, imagination, and pure logic to the rest of the story. All Norwegians who are descendants of Vikings know it to be a fact, that it is not only possible, but actually it is probable that a healthy Viking would sire a child at age 100 and beyond.

So hereafter, please preface any personal salutations to me with the words, "YOUR EXCELLENCY."

Notes:

Historians of Viking history believe that the Moahaugane tumuluses (mounds) in the Vik area, were constructed in 300-400 AD. Construction of similar tumuluses continued into the Viking age (AD 800-1000). It is estimated that each tumulus was considered sacred ground and required about 600 man/days to complete. These burial mounds continued during pagan times until Christian burial practices became customary after 1000 AD.

Archivists in Vik stated, *"Hopperstad was a powerful farm in the middle ages in 'Flatbygdi' in the Vik village. The Hopperstad stave church is estimated to have been built in 1130 AD and is the oldest of the 28 stave churches remaining in Norway today."*

Chapter Three

The Self Made Man

When my grandfather, Ole Johnson, emigrated from Sykkylven, Norway in 1888 his voyage included sailing the ocean on a 3-masted ship; he then took a long train ride finally ending at Wells, Minnesota. He walked westward on Highway 9 (now state-aid Highway 16) carrying his satchel containing all his earthly belongings plus the 75 cents left in his pocket which was all that remained from the money he had saved for the trip.

It has always been the custom since very early times in Norway to freely welcome foot-traveling strangers, because walking had been necessary and so common for persons in Norway who needed to travel distances. Like Ole on this day, travelers in Norway would need to pause for rest and refreshments, or perhaps to spend the night, at unknown homes along the way. In Norway it would have been quite unusual to refuse hospitality to a traveling stranger's needs.

Ole had come to a white house that was the home of Ole and Britha Iverson, which was located quite close by the road with the red barn across on the south side of the road. It was common for farm houses and barns to be located in this manner in Norway, often close to the road so they could enjoy the convenience of the main road close-by; also it was with his convenience in mind that this farmstead had been purposefully designed by Ole Iverson just like farms in Norway.

Britha Iverson normally baked bread for her family twice a week and in times of favorable weather, she would cool the loaves of bread outside on the south window sill.

One day, shortly after they had built this house, a group of Indians came walking on the road. They smelled the wonderful aroma of the fresh-baked bread on the windowsill and inquired of Britha if they could eat some bread. Britha obliged them and the appreciative Indians gave Britha seeds for her garden in exchange for the refreshing fresh baked bread. Britha now had Indian friends, which was of benefit to the Iversons, since this occurred near the time of the famous Indian Uprising in southern Minnesota in 1862.

Like those Indians years before, Ole, being thirsty and hungry from his 20-mile walk, could not miss seeing the fresh baked bread cooling on the windowsill and smell that same tantalizing aroma that the Indians had smelled years before. Remembering the customs of welcoming foot-travelers in Norway, it was natural for Ole to inquire of Britha Iverson if he could enjoy some of that bread. It took little time for Britha to realize that this handsome foot-traveling lad was from Norway, so he was immediately invited into the Iverson home for a meal.

The story of that meal lives on in our family to be told often. Ole is said to have eaten a whole loaf of fresh baked bread with plum jam on that first day. It is an obvious part of the story that he noticed the next to the youngest Iverson daughter, Martha, since eventually she became my grandmother.

The Iversons had a family of 5 daughters and one son at that time. During the 29 years since the Iversons had decided to become homesteading pioneers, they had survived indescribable hardships. The fact that they had conceived 11 children, but only 6 survived, tells only a small part of the story of their many difficult times.

I believe it is appropriate that I call my grandfather the "self-made man" because of his sheer determination to become an American and no longer a Norwegian from the Old Country. He had a sincere goal to work hard, to do everything the right way and to become a success, and this goal was imprinted indelibly on his very soul.

When Ole arrived in New York and the immigration officials asked what his name was, unlike the answer of his brother, Jens Aasen, he chose not to say "Ole Aasen". He had thought about his name during the long days on board the ship before he arrived. By then he had made up his mind that, in his opinion, Aasen was an Old World name and was not an American name. Although there was no one named John in his immediate family, he had definitely made his decision. He answered the immigration official and declared that his name was *"Ole Johnson"*.

His brother, Jens, kept the Aasen name and eventually began farming in North Dakota. Ole, the self-made man, was totally determined to become an American with an American name.

I often think about his name-change, because my mother of German descent often said that she would never have married my father if his name was Aasen. So then where would I be in the whole scheme of things? Take just a moment to contemplate that unanswerable question.

Ole Johnson's first job was to work for a farmer on the farm we once knew as the 'Donald More farm' when I was a lad. However, I don't know the name of the farmer who lived there at that time and hired Ole as a farm hand. I was told that this farmer was a county commissioner and his wife was a schoolteacher. Ole asked the schoolteacher to help him with his English in the evenings. This self-made man was determined to speak the English language properly, a task that usually is impossible for most immigrants from Norway. He succeeded. Unlike his brother, Jens, his English bore no hint of a Norwegian accent, thanks to this teacher and Ole's determination. My father exaggerated that the accent of his Uncle Jens was so thick that you could cut it with a hatchet.

Ole married Martha Iverson on July 1, 1893. They built a farmstead next door to the Iverson farmstead and many years later it became my home. Ole erected a white house, a red barn, a wooden silo, a cattle shed, a hog shed, a chicken house, a corncrib and a machine shed.

Ole and Martha Johnson.

The white house had a back entry between the house and the "summer kitchen." The summer kitchen was a common building for early settlers. It was an unheated room in the winter and used in the summer for cooking, washing and all the other jobs that otherwise would tend to make the main house warmer on the sultry summer days. The wood-burning cookstove in the kitchen ceased

The Ole Johnson farm house (after removal of summer-kitchen on right.)

to be fired-up during the warmest months of the summer, thus keeping the unairconditioned uninsulated home a bit cooler.

Ole intended always to do everything proper, to work hard and become successful. His crops and his livestock always were to be admired. He loved horses. He designed his barn with stalls for 10 horses and 8 cows, so it is easy to see which he most admired.

Since even before he married, he owned a lovely bay mare named Lady that he used between the shafts of his black buggy that sat two people in the single seat. At those times the especially well-to-do farmers had double-seated buggies pulled by a team of two horses. Some of these two-seated buggies had a top with a decorative fringe. The horse harnesses were adorned with splashy white rings, brass knobs on the collar and sometimes bells that created attention as they drove down the street.

Ole's single buggy did not look that impressive, yet everyone turned to look at his rig pulled by Lady when Ole would drive down the main street of Blue Earth. It could aptly be described as being the same as seeing a bright yellow convertible Corvette travel with the top down on Main Street today. It was Lady that every one could not help but notice. Lady would put on a show. She would arch her neck and hold her head high with her ears perked forward. Her nostrils were dilated, and her tail stuck almost straight back. Her front knees raised high with each step and the sound of her hoofs on the cobblestone street entertained everyone who would see Ole driving by. Ole was proud of Lady and loved her as his most favorite horse ever.

Joseph Johnson showing one of his father's horses (perhaps "Lady"?)

The other horses in Ole's barn were all large beautiful Belgian workhorses. Ole was proud of his horses and loved working with them in the fields. Colts would be 2 years old before they were "broke" (trained) to pull. To break a 2-year-old, Ole would use the

2-row corn cultivator in the summer. Four horses side by side pulled the cultivator. The 2-year-old would be put in one of the center slots with 3 other well-trained horses. It would not take long for the young horse to learn to pull like the horses on each side. Ole cultivated all his corn at least 3 and sometimes 4 times each summer. He would "cross-cultivate" (across the planted rows) at least once.

IHC introduced the "Mogul," their lightweight tractor in 1912.

It was 1912 when the news broke all around the neighborhood that Teddy Weber had bought a "Mogul" tractor. All the neighbors sooner or later came to see Teddy plow with the first tractor in the neighborhood. It was a large, dull green, cast iron machine with red wheels, which had sharp steel lugs for traction. It used a 30 gallon gasoline or kerosene tank on top of the machine along with a huge stovepipe exhaust.

Ole was not impressed. His first conclusion was that the Mogul was "so clumsy". He observed that when Teddy turned around on the end of the field row, he would need to leave a 'headland' unplowed that was at least twice as wide as Ole would with his Belgian horses.

Ole quietly told others that day, that with his horses, he could do better than that clumsy 'thing' that burned smelly fuel, smoked, and belched loud noises. Ole told that as he plowed with horses, he could sometimes even hear the meadowlark call. He scoffed as he wondered why anyone would be stupid enough to use a machine like the Mogul to plow, instead of using horses. *"Remember"*, he said, *"my horses are able to respond to my words"*.

One summer years later, Ole had a two-year-old colt that needed 'breaking' He was a beautiful Belgian, but he was different from all the other colts that Ole had raised, because this colt had such huge feet. They were as big as dishpans, according to Ole. To begin his training, the colt was harnessed to the 4-horse corn cultivator with 3 other well-trained horses. The colt was so clumsy with those big feet, that he seemed to place them on each and every corn plant as they turned at the end to return in the opposite direction. Only a few plants at the end of the field were left standing where they turned. That's why the colt with the big feet forever became named "Mogul." It was a loving name, but not very complimentary.

Mogul was a gentle horse. All the grandchildren got to ride him when he was taken from the barn to the water tank to drink. His back was so broad that it seemed that our feet stood straight out on each side when we were on top. I remember walking home after school from District 97 on February 22, 1941, and arriving at Grandpa's place just as his farm sale was auctioning the horses. It was sad to see Mogul go. Grandpa had retired from farming and was moving to their new home in Blue Earth, MN.

While he farmed, his eight cows had always been milked by hand every day, twice a day. Each evening Ole would carry the fresh milk from the cow barn to the DeLaval cream separator in the separator house nearby. I only remember his new separator, which was powered by an electric motor. Previously, the separator had a crank on the side, which required both hands to turn the wide crank handle. For the cream separator to function properly, it had to be turned at just the correct speed. Ole would pour the milk into the strainer at the top of the separator milk bowl. The milk would slowly run down into the turning plates of the separator and the separated cream would slowly run out of the top spout into a tall cream can. The skim milk would come out of the lower spout a bit faster into a larger pail and was later fed to the chickens and pigs. The tall, covered cream can was partially filled when it was lowered with a rope through a trap door into the damp well-pit below the windmill to be cooled until the next day.

The following morning after milking Ole would bring up the partially filled can of cream from the well-pit and place it under the top cream separator spout again to add that morning's newly separated cream to almost fill the tall cream can.

Then came Ole's favorite time of the day and it happened every day. Ole would go to the horse barn to curry and comb Lady's hair and then harness her to the single buggy. After placing the tall cream can behind the buggy seat, he would drive Lady down the driveway and turn right on the road as he passed the mailbox. Ole and Lady would go one-half mile north to the farm of Irv Grout. Irv would be waiting and would set his tall can of cream beside Ole's. Ole and Lady would then drive back south towards home with Lady performing her showy natural attributes all the way. As they passed the Johnson driveway at the mailbox, unlike most other horses, Lady did not attempt a return to the barn.

She didn't need to because she had done this so often that she knew exactly where she needed to go. She held her head high as she passed the mail box and continued with a natural trotting pace one half-mile south to the Miller Creamery. Ole would stop by the loading dock and unload the two cans of cream. The buttermaker would weigh each can, dump it, steam it and reweigh the can. After setting the cans on the loading dock, he would write the weights in his ledger and determine the weight of the cream for each farmer.

Then Ole and Lady would head north and trot right past the Johnson driveway and mailbox the second time. Again unlike most horses, she did not need to return to the barn. Rather she went right on past to continue to Irv Grout's farm. After leaving Irv's empty cream can, Ole and Lady would return toward home. Now, at last Lady knew her job was done, so this time she turned in the driveway without Ole needing to steer with the reins. Lady had been well trained and knew the daily routine perfectly. She stopped in front of the barn like always and waited to be unharnessed and take a drink of water from the stock tank south of the barn.

On the trip one day Ole had informed Irv Grout and the buttermaker that he was going to try an experiment. He suspected that Lady knew the routine so well that it would be fun to see if she could deliver the cream to the buttermaker and the empty can to Irv Grout without a driver on the next day.

So the next day Ole put his filled cream can in the back of the buggy, tied the reins loosely to the buggy whip and said, "Giddap, Lady." Lady trotted down the driveway and turned north to go to the Grout farm. There Irv put his can of cream beside Ole's can and said, "Giddap, Lady." Lady went south right past the mailbox at home without turning to go to the barn. She pulled up at the loading ramp at the creamery just like always and stopped. The buttermaker weighed the cans, steamed them, reweighed them, marked the weight down and placed the empty cans in the back of the buggy. Then the buttermaker said, "Giddap, Lady." Lady turned the buggy around and headed north to deliver the empty can to the Grout farm. She trotted right by the farm again as Ole proudly watched her from a distance. Lady delivered the empty can just like always and then returned home to stop where she always did to be unharnessed and watered again.

From that day forward, Lady delivered the cream from the two farms every morning alone without a driver until she was no longer able. One morning when Ole went out to the barn, Lady was in trouble. She was old. She was not able to stand on her rear feet. She struggled but only could rise on her front feet. She was too weak.

Ole knew what had to be done, but he was unable to do it. He called Irv Grout to come with his gun. Ole went into his bedroom in the house for a long long time. Irv came and left. There was one task that the self-made man was completely unable to do.

Chapter Four

Back in the Old Country

U ncle Jens and I had immediately established a mutual-admiration-society as soon as he came to live with us for a year or so. Jens Aasen was a brother to my grandfather, Ole Johnson. At that time in 1933 Jens was seventy years old and I was five. Uncle Jens came to our farm with four handsome Belgian farm horses and the most beautiful 1930 Model A Ford I had ever seen. Unlike all the other Fords I had seen, this automobile was a shiny brown color with shiny black fenders. After Jens arrived, his Ford never left our farm with only one occupant since Jens always took this 5-year-old along. We soon became inseparable pals.

My grandparents, Ole and Martha Johnson lived on the farm about a quarter of a mile west

Jens Aasen (1934.)

of the original Iverson farmstead where we lived when Uncle Jens came to live with us. Both farm sites were on land that was a portion of the original Iverson homestead which was first settled by my great grand-father, Ole Iverson, in 1861.

Aasen home in Norway (some time after Ole and Jens left.)

Although Jens and Ole both immigrated from Norway in 1888, Ole had decided that Aasen was too much of an "old world" name, so when he arrived, he changed his name to Ole Johnson even though there didn't happen to be any previous Aasens named "John" to normally make the name traditional.

I later found out that it was fortuitous that Ole's name was changed to "Johnson" which automatically made my name, Johnson, because my German-descended mother, Elsie Alma Fenske, had said that she would never have married my father had his name been Aasen. So then, where would I be in the great grand scheme of everything?

Jens Aasen's North Dakota Farm.

Shortly after immigrating, Jens Aasen traveled farther west and bought a farm in Barton, North Dakota where farms had larger acreages per farm than in Minnesota. Jens' farming endeavor did not go as well as he had hoped. The dust bowl, the hungry grasshopper swarms and the Great Depression in the early 1930's, dealt harsh blows to farmers in North Dakota. Money wasn't produced when rains didn't come and crops didn't grow.

Jens's wife, Anna Lindvick, had immigrated from the Norfjord area in Norway and had been his loving helpmate during their years on their wind-swept, almost treeless farm, but she died childless in 1927. I cannot begin to imagine the multiple sadnesses that Jens experienced in 1933 as he sold everything but his four horses and his beautiful Model A Ford. Sadly, he left North Dakota forever to come to live with us in Minnesota. He loved living with us, he loved me, and he was our beloved "Uncle Jens."

When Uncle Jens came, our barn was totally occupied with livestock, including our horses, milk cows and calves, so there was no place for Uncle Jens' four horses. My father and Uncle Jens felled several cottonwood trees and had them sawed into planks at a sawmill near Frost, MN. Using cottonwood planks, they attached a temporary lean-to horse barn to the north side of our red barn. It was just large enough to protect the horses from the wind and snow through the winter until spring. I'm sure that Dad and Uncle Jens considered that, by delaying the sale of the horses that fall and instead feeding and protecting them over winter, it would be financially beneficial to Uncle Jens. They rightly assumed that the early spring market for draft horses would improve when the farmers who might need extra draft horses would become eager to start preparing for the new crop season.

They didn't wake me, but on a beautiful autumn evening toward midnight, Uncle Jens came downstairs and awakened my Dad saying, *"Joe, we better go out to the barn and check my horses. I think I hear the horses fighting."*

They both dressed and, upon going out to that lean-to horse barn, discovered the horses were just fine. The noise actually was coming from the neighbor a half mile west who had just finished building a new round-roofed barn that summer and decided to invite all their friends from Blue Earth to celebrate with a rollicking barn dance in that large empty haymow. So try to imagine what might have been happening in that celebration that was loud enough to wake Uncle Jens in his upstairs bedroom a half-mile away, because it sounded like horses fighting.

Perhaps it was about 12 years later when I was 17 years old that I discovered remnants of that celebration in the haymow of that barn. I was part of the grain threshing crew that August. I had never before seen the inside of that barn, so during lunch break, being curious, I climbed up into the haymow and found in a dusty corner, a pile of electric cables with many red and green bulbs. Surely these strings of lights had decorated the empty haymow at the big barn dance that night 12 years ago, but I assume had never been returned to the rightful owner.

At Christmas time each year, the city of Blue Earth would hang long strings of these rather large red and green bulbs with pine garlands above and across the main street going from corner to corner at the center of each intersection. I now knew how that barn dance was lit and adorned on the night that Uncle Jens in his bedroom a half mile away thought he heard the horses fighting.

At age 17 for the first time, I was proud to have my own 'bundle team' of horses and hayrack to haul the shocked oat bundles from the field to the cattle yard and pitch them into the belt-driven threshing machine. This separated the oats from the straw, which was blown into a large pile in the cattle yard. The straw-pile provided shelter for cattle not housed in the barn. From time to time straw was carried into the barn to be used for livestock bedding.

This neighborhood cooperative harvest serviced each farm in our close neighborhood with each farmer furnishing a man with a team of horses and hayrack to bring the bundles from the field. A "thresher meeting" was held each year before the season to decide the order of the farms to be harvested. Normally, each year they would start on the opposite end of the neighborhood, from what they did the year previous. The tractor and threshing machine were owned by my father. The cost of the machine and my father's labor operating the machine was announced and agreed upon at the meeting.

As a youth, I looked forward to threshing time as a time of fun working with the neighbors and consuming enormous wonderful meals prepared by the housewives on each farm. Of course, the older men never admitted that there was any purpose for threshing other than work, yet I know that everyone enjoyed that time together. I suppose at the time, I was perhaps the only person that would admit openly that I eagerly looked forward to this special social event each summer.

Alvin Erickson and his grain bundle wagon at threshing time.

The afternoon lunches were served daily at 3:00 PM from a children's coaster wagon pulled out near the threshing machine which did not even slow down for a lunch break. After each 'bundle wagon' was completely unloaded, the driver would have time for a quick break for a glass or two of cold pink lemonade with sandwiches and perhaps a piece of cake. The work and hot weather at that time each August was easily accepted, because this was the social event of the summer which made hard work fun.

I have always loved the threshing time because it was so special; especially so on the year that I had become a member of the threshing crew with my own "bundle team" for the first time. It was a time to celebrate since it perhaps was my right of passage of childhood into manhood.

It was while threshing grain that year that I sneaked into the haymow and saw a dusty pile of lights that brought back fond memories of Uncle Jens, who on a late night suspected that his Belgian horses needed his attention, only to realize there was a barn dance.

He had been my loving Uncle Jens who cared for me and thought I was special. By this time Uncle Jens was no longer alive, and it was good to remember again a special story about a special person in my childhood as I looked upon a dusty pile of lights in the corner of a haymow.

One doesn't recall very many things that happened at age 5, so the few incidents that I fondly recall include Uncle Jens who took me along everywhere he went in his Model A Ford. One day on the way from our farm to Frost, MN, we had a small accident. At that time Model A Fords were surely not required to use commercial child seats. I suspect that perhaps seat belts for cars were yet to be invented. I always STOOD in front of the passenger seat with my hands or arms on the slight dashboard. After a spring rain the country road, more dirt than gravel, was slippery. Somehow we slid into the slight ditch on the right side of the road and the beautiful Ford was no longer upright, but was lying on its right side. The last thing I remember is seeing the mud puddle ahead, but I have no memory of how we got out of the car. The next thing I remember was that Uncle Jens became so excited, not because of the condition of the car, but because I had a small bleeding gash on my forehead. Seeing my red blood immediately changed Uncle Jens. He was devastated. He knew he had made a mistake by neglecting his responsibility to keep this five-year-old safe from harm.

Fortunately, the next vehicie to come by was a truck with at least four Mexican sugar beet farm workers. They made swift work of setting the Ford upright again. In my memory I don't think the Ford was damaged at all. The slow motion fall into the grass and soft dirt tested those solid fenders, but I believe that they were not even dented. Uncle Jens turned the Ford around and we hurried home to my mother to decide what to do with the bleeding boy. Mother poured a bit of Lysol into the warm water to wash the small cut and a gauze bandage was applied. Uncle Jens was finally relieved when the red blood was out of sight, but continued to feel badly because he was so fond of me. After the accident whenever I rode in the beautiful brown Ford with Uncle Jens, I was instructed, "*Sit down on the seat*".

While they lived and farmed near Barton, N.D. Uncle Jens and his wife Anna informally adopted or fostered a child, Borghild, who needed a home. Borghild later became Mrs. A.W. Loss and her descendants presently live in the area near Minnewaukan, ND.

One year during their farming years in North Dakota Anna became homesick and desperately wanted to see the family she had left in Norway. Jens and Anna decided that she should go back to visit.

Jens and Ole had an older sister, Karolina Aasen, who never left Norway and never married. She had remained her whole lifetime living alone in the Aasen family two-room home until age 85. It was half-way up the mountain above the village of Sykkylven. Karolina grew and ground her own wheat for flour, sheared her sheep, spun the wool, milked the cow, gave the neighbors butter and fetched her water from the flowing well carrying two pails using her carved wooden neck-yoke.

Jens and Ole discussed Anna's trip back to Norway and together decided that Anna should bring a gift to Karolina from her brothers in America. Ole purchased a wooden hanging wall clock with a carved horse at the top from the Elwin More Jewelry store in Blue Earth, Minnesota, for Anna to deliver to Karolina whom she had never previously met.

Anna had a concern that she contemplated as she traveled across the ocean. Since Karolina had never known Anna, she was concerned that if she at first would introduce herself as Jens' wife perhaps the first thought that Karolina might have is that she is about to hear an announcement of grave news about her brothers which might cause her to immediately become terribly upset. Anna chose her words carefully and practiced them. When Karolina came to answer the door, this is what Anna said. *"Do you have relatives in America?"* After Karolina answered that she had two brothers, Ole and Jens, in America, Anna introduced herself that she was the wife of Jens. She then delivered the attractive wall clock with the horse on the top and which had an engraved brass plate near the bottom that read, "To Karolina, from her brothers Jens and Ole - Elwin Moore Jewelry, Blue Earth, Minnesota".

Victor and Eleanor showing Caroline's clock in Aasen.

When Uncle Jens told my parents and me about where he lived and what it was like in Norway, he always began the story with the words, *"Back in the old country"*. Then would come a story in his accented English language, which was often interspersed with Norwegian words. As a young boy I became totally fascinated with Norway and the people there and hoped that someday I could go there to see the place where my grandparents and Uncle Jens left to immigrate to America.

Because that early desire to see Norway never diminished, I have taken three wonderful Norwegian trips *"back in the old counry"*. It has been imperative on each trip that we visit the small two-room home half-way up the mountain above Sykkylven. I assure you that the pendulum wooden wall clock topped with the small horse still clicks away on the wall of the main room in the tiny home that Ole and Jens left to come to America while their sister Karolina spent her entire life living in that home with the pine floor, which Uncle Jens told that they scrubbed with lye water to keep the cleaned floor a light color.

Now when I think back, it is remarkable that at age five I had had a total fascination with two subjects, Norway and airplanes. When I think about it now, this seems unusual considering that this was at a time when all the farmers in our neighborhood were still farming with horses, and automobiles had been on the dirt roads less than 20 years at the time. From time to time whenever an airplane would occasionally fly over our home, I would run outside, point to the sky and shout, *"airplane, airplane."* It must have happened often because Uncle Jens realized that I loved airplanes. At the time, like many who preceded me, I could only imagine flying in the sky like a bird totally unleashed from the restraints of gravity. These airplane incidents completely captured the fresh imagination and desires of this 5-year-old farm child.

For my birthday in August, Uncle Jens gave me a three-wheeled pedal airplane with a steerable rear wheel. I could pedal it around in the farmyard. It had a white star on the wing and a propellor that didn't go around much, only when I leaned over the steering wheel and gave it a swift push. It was painted army green and on its side it read, "Army Scout Plane". It was a bit easier to pedal on the gravel driveway than in the grass lawn.

Victor's airplane gift from Uncle Jens Aasen.

Now as I think of it, Uncle Jens gave a mighty gift to me during the Great Depression when money was scarce. He had given up all of his farming property in North Dakota and now lived, not at a place of his own, but with loving relatives. For a child during the Great Depression, it was by far the best gift I could ever have received. Indeed Uncle Jens loved me and yes, that began a life-long love of flying; indeed much later in my life, I generously fulfilled that early dream by actually flying my "second" airplane to many places in the North American continent, criss-crossing the lower 48 states to its four corners and even flying to Alaska, Canada, and Abaco, Bahama.

Grandfather Ole was so determined to put away everything from *"back in the old country"* that he asked for tutored help and worked diligently to be able to talk like other Minnesotans without a trace of Norwegian accent.

Uncle Jens talked with a Norwegian accent and often forgot to speak the English language as he automatically switched into Norwegian. My father understood the Norwegian language, so Uncle

Jens often did not bother to try to speak English. I was fascinated with his foreign language that I could not understand. It made me want to learn much more about the real place that I often pictured in my mind that was *"back in the old country,"* and I have never recovered. That two-room log cabin wall remains today adorned with a beloved clock with a carved horse doing what clocks have always been meant to do.

This 5-year-old followed Uncle Jens whenever and wherever Uncle Jens helped my father with the farm work and the conversation always seemed to turn to Sykkylven, Norway. Then Uncle Jens began his fond remembrances with the words, "Back in the old country" and the story would proceed as he would explain to my father and me all about what it was like in Norway. Day after day my father and I would learn more about that place, "back in the old country". My imagination soared to that far-away place across the ocean as I learned more each day about Norway. His stories whetted my desire to some day investigate that place and that heritage that Ole and Jens had left to take a big chance in a "new country". I have never completed the impossible quest to learn all I wanted to know about Norway, even after three trips to Norway in 1981, 1999 and 2007 to visit that beautiful scenery with wonderful relatives, who make the knowledge of my heritage so fulfilling. The imaginary Norway of my childhood became real and I was so fortunate to learn to love those people that live "back in the old country". These beautiful memories will last forever in my recollections and like Uncle Jens, I can tell stories any time, even if I'm not asked, about *Back in the Old Country*.

Chapter Five

The Banker

Many Sunday afternoons were spent with my parents and grandparents as we often visited Grandma Emma and Grandpa W.D. Fenske on Sundays at their home in Blue Earth. As a hyperactive child, I would become bored with the adult conversation and lack of activity. I needed activity. It was not natural for me to sit still on a sunny Sunday afternoon. I would bring my steel clamp-on roller skates with the leather strap around the ankle and skate all around the block for several hours. I loved to skate on the side-walks in town. Unlike any place on our farm with the gravel and grass and lack of smooth places to skate, the concrete sidewalks were marvelous for skating. For me, it was joy and great fun.

I would feel the need to satisfy my hunger at about 3:00 PM. The Sunday noon lunch had all been worked off. I knew the usual routine. When I would come in, Grandma Emma would go to her purse with the two little metal knobs on the top and would retrieve a 25 cent coin. Then she would tell my dad, *"Joe, why don't you go to the corner grocery store and get some ice cream?"* At that time everyone knew that a pint of ice cream cost 25 cents. Dad knew she liked the kind with the three different colors, chocolate, vanilla, and strawberry. When he returned, she would open the carton and carefully cut as many slices as there were people in the room. I was terribly dismayed when more people showed up for the coffee hour at Grandma's house because then the slices of ice cream became terribly thin. Usually Grandma would add one vanilla wafer on the side of the slice of ice cream. On the days she had no vanilla wafers with the lovely white filling, to my dismay she would substitute a white soda cracker to go with the slice of ice cream.

Grandma Emma's cousin, Walter Oelke, and his wife came on one of those Sundays when the ice cream was sliced really thin. To make conversation, Grandma Emma asked Walter, *"You always raise a lot of potatoes in your garden. With the drought being so bad, how are your potatoes doing?"* Walter with a straight face and a really deep bass voice replied, *"Oh, my potatoes are doing really good. You know, I plant every other row onions between every row of potatoes. Then I have plenty of moisture. The onions make the potatoes' eyes water."* Grandma Emma who never seemed to have a sense of humor, without a smile replied in her German accent, *"Augh, I don' believe dot."*

Family Christmas was always celebrated by the children and grandchildren gathering on an afternoon at Grandma and Grandpa Fenske's house during the holiday season to exchange Christmas gifts. Grandma Emma always seemed to relish the idea that she was "sickly". In fact she claimed to be so sick at the time my father and mother were to marry that my parents' wedding date was moved up hurriedly and was held in the Fenske living room so Grandma would still be "alive" at their wedding. She always claimed that she would die soon, but in spite of her miscalculations, she lived until I became a teenager.

Like clock-work in the midst of the excitement at every annual family Christmas gathering, Grandma Emma would go to the top drawer in the dining room buffet and from her purse with the two opposed metal buttons at the top, she would retrieve 10 half-dollar coins, one for each of her grandchildren. Then came her annual proclamation as she gave a coin to each child, *"Now remember, this may be the last gift you will ever get from me, because I don't think I will live to be here next Christmas."* We all had heard this same litany year after year. In spite of her annual claim, she really remained quite healthy and for many years enjoyed this Christmas gathering with her family.

Grandma's house had a gravity-fed furnace in the basement. The heat circulated up through the big floor register located in the exact center of the small square house. In the winter everyone would stand over the register to warm up after being out in the cold of winter. On this particular year, Grandma Emma had made the dire prediction of her demise and had given each of us our half-dollar coin. My older cousin, Dennis, accidentally let the half-dollar slip from his hand. He looked down as he watched it disappear into the dark depths of oblivion into the bowels of the furnace below. Every one laughed as Dennis proclaimed, *"OOPS, there goes my nickel."* Grandma retrieved another coin from her purse in the top buffet drawer and sternly admonished Dennis, *"Now don't drop this one."*

Grandma Emma was always capable of pronouncing moral judgment on persons who she thought were doing something that in her opinion she had determined was not acceptable. She would go on and on about those people and it seemed she often repeated the same criticism about the same persons on subsequent Sunday afternoons.

One of the often 'offenders' were the Kallestad girls who lived directly across the street. As I recall, the Kallestads had 5 or 7 daughters and most of these young ladies were at the age that interested young lads would come to pick them up in the evening and return them quite late in the night according to Grandma. She would watch them out of her front bay window each night to keep an account of how late they came home and how often they went out. With that many eligible girls in the Kallestad household, Grandma Emma was kept busy passing judgment on their terrible behavior as she watched them night after night, but since this often happened on Saturday nights, she could relay her conclusions of suspect behavior to us the following Sunday afternoon. She said that it was so bad because no good can come of girls that go out that often and stay out that late. She even thought it was terrible that some of the girls went out with different guys on different nights; they didn't even stay with the same fellow. At that time I was much younger than the Kallestad girls. I was still at the age of roller-skating around the block. At my young age, I had learned that the Kallestad girls must be really bad because Grandma had said so. She would often admonish her grandchildren that they should never behave badly like the Kallestad girls. Now when I consider her complaints, there seemed to be no acceptable time for fellows and young ladies to be together after dark before marriage. For these young ladies to be going out *"so late"* at night and not be married was totally unacceptable behavior according to Grandma Emma.

Because these times were during the throes of the Depression, the dealings of Banker John Domes at the Blue Earth State Bank kindled Grandma's judgmental ire on a number of Sunday afternoons. The Depression time was difficult since money was scarce for everyone. The "bank holiday" was still fresh in the minds of all that had lost money in the bank when it "closed". When the banks opened again, it opened without the customers' deposits. Personal savings and regular business funds had been swallowed up in the Great Depression. Grandma Emma proclaimed that one should never trust the banks or the bankers again.

She named banker John Domes as the worst of the bankers since he had foreclosed the mortgages of a number of farmers that Grandma Emma knew. She said that John Domes is rich now that he *"took their farm"* when these friends were unable to make the mortgage payments.

It was simple for the banker; if you didn't pay the annual mortgage payment, the contract provides that the foreclosed farm then is owned by the bank and John Domes owned the bank. Because of Grandma Emma, I thought that John Domes had to be the most awful man in the country. Why, he now had *"stolen"* 4 farms from Grandma's acquaintances. The next week she would give a new count perhaps 5 or 6 farms that John Domes had *"stolen"* from their hard-working friends. At my young age I was impressed with the dereliction of that awful banker, John Domes. There must not be a meaner, more awful man in Blue Earth. I visualized him with horns, a fork in his hand and a black tail. He was really bad. I knew because Grandma had said so.

Many times my father would transport Grandma and Grandpa Fenske to our farm home for Sunday dinner. I don't think Grandma Emma ever dared to drive a car and Grandpa Fenske seldom drove especially as he eventually grew older.

Grandpa Fenske always wore his gray suit with a vest on Sunday. There he sat after dinner in the rocking chair in the corner of our living room, casually rocking. At about 3:30 PM he would stop rocking and would take the engraved gold watch from his vest pocket. That impressive gold watch was attached to a sturdy gold chain that looped through the center buttonhole of his vest. It was impressive jewelry. He would push the knob at the top of the watch to make the cover pop open and he would then read the time. He would grunt, "Ough", close the watch cover and return the gold piece to its rightful pocket in his vest. Minutes later he would repeat the performance of taking the watch out, pushing the knob to open the cover, check the time, close the cover and grunt, *"Ough"* again as he returned the big gold watch to its rightful place in his vest pocket. This performance complete with the accompanying *"Ough"* was repeated several times until it was exactly 20 minutes before 4 in the afternoon. Then Grandpa Fenske would announce, *"Joe, you better take us home. I have to feed the chickens."*

Grandfather Fenske kept chickens in town in a small fenced-in enclosure on the back side of his one-car garage. His narrow chicken "coop" had a roost and several nests for the 6 or 8 hens he kept for their daily supply of fresh eggs. Each afternoon at precisely 4 PM Grandfather would strew the daily supply of "scratch grain" on the ground for the chickens. Scratch grain consisted of oats and cracked corn.

Upon Grandpa's request, my father would drive them back to their home in Blue Earth. The pleasure of the Sunday dinner at our home and the social afternoon with Grandpa and Grandma always came to an end at precisely 3:40 PM on the days they came to our house for Sunday dinner.

W.D. Fenske retired from active farming shortly after he had caught his hand in the husking-bed rollers of a horse-drawn corn picker. I remember not his left hand, only a wrist, since his left hand had been amputated.

After climbing the crowded stairs, the third story attic of the Fenske home was a really good place for me to escape and play, sometimes accompanied by my cousins. We cousins found a fascinating hand prosthesis consisting of a laced leather tube to which was attached a very solid and immovable gloved hand. The gloved hand could be screwed off and replaced with a hook, not unlike Captain Hook's menacing hook in the comics. It was an impressive item when used to pretend to be a pirate. I still remember those creative games as a young lad pretending that we might be imaginary pirates in the attic of Grandpa's house.

W.D. and Emma Fenske (some time after his hand was amputated.)

Horse drawn corn picker.

I asked Grandpa why he didn't ever wear his artificial hand. He said, *"It is nothing but a nuisance."*

W.D. Fenske was a very successful farmer as retired farmers were thought of in those days. Anyone who could "set up" his sons each with a farm as he retired was considered quite successful. He had indeed set up each of his three sons with a farm consisting of a quarter section or 160 acres. Since W.D. had immigrated from Germany as a youth, I will attempt to describe my Grandpa in terms of my own making, that I thought to be apt descriptive terminology of the kind of person that was W.D. Fenske. I called him a "Kaiser-Wilhelm German," one who demanded that all things be done *"My way, right now."* That's how Grandpa W. D. seemed to me. All his life, Grandpa Fenske had risen really early each morning, worked hard, and demanded that everything be done properly and promptly by all in his household including himself. He was a firm direct moral man.

Although he had left his farm to retire to a home in the town of Blue Earth, nevertheless, his interests continued in the occupation of farming, particularly the farming habits of his three sons. Thus he felt he could retain a continuing personal "management interest" in the farms of his sons due to his charitable gift to each of them.

When W.D. would visit his oldest son, Gust, on the farm to give his advice as to how the farming should be done, he got less than a charitable reception. For it's true that Gust, like his father, was also a Kaiser-Wilhelm German who got up at 4 AM to do all the livestock chores before breakfast. After breakfast he would head for the fields in season and I recall that he was proud to declare that he cultivated his corn 5 times, 3 times lengthwise and twice he cross-cultivated (across the rows like a checker-board). Being made of the same Kaiser-Wilhelm German stock as his father, the advice was not always readily acceptable to put it mildly.

Not to be deterred, W.D. would attempt to give some of his well-earned farming advice to his middle son, Marvin, who had been allowed to have the 'home farm' on which W.D. had spent all his years before retirement. Although Marvin also came from Kaiser-Wilhelm German stock, he was a bit mellower because he understood that because he was on the farm that understandably was special to his father, he needed to give credence to his father's advice. Yet when sometimes the advice did not happen to be accepted graciously, W.D. would leave.

It was a whole different approach when W.D. would go to his youngest son's farm to give advice. Harry was not a Kaiser-Wilhelm German. Rather he was an easy going, laid-back pipe-smoker. Harry never seemed to get excited nor was he bothered when things didn't seem to go just right. This was a frustration for W.D. since Harry's relaxed approach would often stretch his father's patience.

One day W.D. came to visit his son as Harry was splitting wood for the wood-burning stove in the kitchen. Obviously Harry was not chopping wood in the manner approved by his father, so he said, *"Augh, you chop wood like a woodpecker; here, give me the axe!"* Although Harry was a grown man, W.D. took the axe from him and with his left stump arm on the chunk of wood and his right hand around the axe-handle, W.D. proceeded to dispatch the split pieces of wood in the slick approved manner in spite of his disability.

To escape his frustration, W.D. often came to our farm to spend time with my father, Joe, his son-in-law. Joe was not a Kaiser-Wilhelm German. In fact he was an agreeable Norwegian.

Besides, W.D. did not have a vested interest in our farm since it required no charity from W.D, so he and my father got along famously. W.D. continued to come to visit and help day after day. W.D. enjoyed the company of my father when he could assist with certain things that made him feel that he had been helpful and of use to us.

We had been required in 1934 to move our house to a new location. Its close proximity to the highway was a problem and the State of Minnesota paid to have the house moved. My father wanted his new basement deep enough to have a 9-foot ceiling. He used a 'slush-bucket' behind a team of horses to dig the basement. A slush-bucket is shaped like a scoop shovel about 3 or 4 feet wide pulled by a team of two horses. It had two handles to be controlled by two strong arms to constantly maintain the depth of the cut as the slush-bucket moved forward and filled. I remember my father walking behind with the leather reins to steer the horses tied over his shoulder and under one arm. When the bucket was full, Dad would push the handles down and the horses would skid the full load of soil up the ramp to the dirt pile. To dump the slush-bucket, he needed to briskly lift the handles upward to cause the slush-bucket to roll upside-down as the horses were moving forward.

August Egeness came with his steam engine to move the house over the newly dug basement-hole. When the house was in place and standing on temporary pilings, the masons came to build the foundation basement walls. The basement was built according to my father's design since he required a 9-foot ceiling, so he could swing an axe without striking the ceiling. Thereafter one-half of that basement was annually filled with wood to be burned in the new house furnace in the basement.

One day W.D. Fenske was helping my father as he split wood in that new deep basement. This was the conversation:

W.D.: *"Joe, you've been awfully quiet lately. Is there something wrong?"*

Joe: (quietly after a significant pause) *"No."*

W.D.: (After another significant pause) *"Joe, don't you have a farm payment coming due pretty soon at the bank?"*

Joe: (after another pause) *"Ya."*

W.D.: *"How much is it, Joe?"*

Joe: *"$300."*

W.D.: *"Do you know where you're going to get it?"*

Joe: (really softly) *"No."*

W.D.: *"Well Joe, I've got $300 if you want to use it."*

With $300 in hand, my father proceeded to the Blue Earth State Bank to face the infamous John Domes. He put the cash on the marble top of the bank counter in front of John Domes. Mr. Domes turned his head down to see the cash lying there. He spoke, *"Where did you get that?"* My father who has been noted for his one-liners responded, *"I robbed a bank."* Then he turned and walked out.

But for that $300 where would I be? Like the great philosopher, Yogi Berra, advised, *"When you come to a fork in the road, take it."*

Chapter Six

The Dell Store

The Dell Store is NOT a computer store, but rather it is a very special, very general store and the "Dell" in which the store is located is precisely as described in the dictionary definition of the word—*"a small secluded valley covered with trees or turf"*.

But "Dell Store" is so much more than a store located at the convergence of valley, river, trees and road located in a lovely wooded setting. The feeble words of this essay will never capture the living flavor and culture of the store, nor can words adequately describe the appreciative feelings of those in the extended neighborhood that were served by the beloved, entertaining and accommodating Norwegian bachelor proprietors, Thoralf and Valdemar (Valdy) Schanke. The store had everything anyone might ever need in those days, and most everything from the barrels was "sold in bulk". The business which began prior to 1900 ceased to exist at the time of Thoralf's death in 1964.

The lovely memories and stories about the store, which can yet be recalled, beg to be recorded and not forgotten, since there are so few "Dell Storytellers" now living who purchased lutefisk from Thoralf or were entertained by Valdy's imagination. The Schanke Store served as the social center of the community for about 80 years together with the Norwegian Lutheran Church across the road, which is still active. It was the parents of the Schanke brothers that started the store only a few decades after the original Norwegian immigration and settlement of the Dell community.

Since I was not there, I can only imagine that on a sunny summer afternoon in 1910, my grandfather, Ole Johnson, who immigrated from Norway in 1888, must have been on his way to Dell for some supplies. He would be driving Lady, his favorite bay horse.

Beside him in his little buggy, sat his son, Joseph, who at that time would have been 15 years old and who one day would become my father.

Trotting east toward the river on the Dell road, they could soon see the bridge which had been built in 1858 among the large deciduous trees surrounding the river on both sides. As they began down the hill, Lady could relax in her harness, because the buggy would be rolling easily down hill and would even push her a bit as they rolled along. They could see the north-south road intersection ahead, but dominating their full view across that road were the steep front steps of the beautiful white Norwegian Lutheran Church with a tall bell tower which had the tallest spire of any church in the area. On the left (north) side of the church was the hitching rail by the cemetery with its white stone markers. The location of this church established in 1871 was meant to be the center of the tiny settlement.

Lady pulled the buggy up a slight incline after crossing the bridge. The "free school" was on the left side of the road and on the right side was the Schanke Dell Store. On the south side of the church was the large white two-story parsonage. Just south of the parsonage was the Egeness blacksmith shop. This road in front of the church, going north and south from Dell parallel to the tree-lined river, led to farm fields and homesteads that had been settled by families of Norwegian descent.

Their destination that day was the Dell Store, on the right side of the buggy as they came to a stop. Joseph tied Lady to the hitching rails handily provided on each side of the front door of the store. There was a slim many-paned window on each side of the front door.

After entering the store, the first item they saw was the Tastee Bread display in front of the chimney which had been erected in the exact center of the room. Beyond the chimney was the pot-bellied stove which provided heat in the cold months. At the base of the chimney and on the floor between the Tastee Bread display and the stove was the well-used spitoon.

The very favorite social gathering place of choice for farmers at the end of the day was beyond the pot-bellied stove in the rear of the store where there were numerous nail kegs, paint pails, and wooden barrels containing food staples such as oatmeal, crackers, apples, herring, smoked or salted fish. Since there were no chairs, the kegs, barrels, and pails provided the seats conveniently located not too far from the pot-bellied stove.

The farmers gathered most every evening to chat, gossip, argue, tell stories, announce weddings, births, deaths, sicknesses, accidents and any other vital statistics. Sometimes this might include heated political arguments and very likely included discussions of various theological issues. Thoralf's special interest was Bible prophesy, and many men would hear his opinion before they left the store. Consuming such essential information would often last long into the evenings while these dedicated Dell Store customers drank pop and non-alcoholic malt, ate candy bars, smoked or chewed tobacco. They ate purchased snacks and shucked the free peanuts from the 100-pound gunny sack, disposing of the cast-off shells conveniently on the floor. These after-work evening gatherings, where anyone was welcome, was a hallmark of the popularity of the Dell Store and often continued on until 11 pm.

In 1910, on the day I imagined that Ole and Joseph came there, the ice cream refrigerator with the fitted round covers at the top would not yet have been there, because electricity was not available until after 1930. In later times Dixie cups, ice cream bars, pints, and hand-dipped ice cream became available for the back-of-the-store evening social gatherings. The record went to Ernie Fenske, who, according to the oft-told story, once ate six or seven ice cream bars.

There always was an unspoken rule that when any customer walked in the front door, all conversations by the social set in the rear of the store became silent. After all, if the "boys" continued their gossiping and storytelling, they would be unable to hear the conversations of Thoralf or Valdy as they assisted the latest customer, who perhaps might even share an extra bit of news while shopping at Dell to be absorbed by the boys.

Imagine a new young housewife who might come for some supplies and this crew of men instantly became stone-silent as she entered with every pair of eyes looking exactly in her direction. It was something to get used to; otherwise she learned to shop earlier in the day before the boys gathered for their evening of sociability.

On the right side of the room, when viewed from the front door, was the counter with the cash register and the brown wrapping paper dispenser which had the large spool of white string at the top. The shelving on the wall behind the counter displayed groceries, canned goods and supplies such as the liniments and patent medicines including a brand named Cutico. There were five-pound boxes of tobacco that a guy would use a jack-knife to cut off a 'hunk' to chew.

On the counter were displayed slabs of bacon, little wooden boxes of smoked herring or salted fish and jars of pickled pigs' feet. At the end of the counter was the large barrel of crackers sold by weight.

Crackers go very well with cheese, so one can ask Valdy to cut off a hunk of cheese from the large round 75-pound chunk, about two feet in diameter near the cracker barrel at the end of the counter. Also on the counter was the large hand-cranked coffee grinder. Coffee beans were taken directly out of the burlap sack or from one of the supply drawers on the back side of the counter. These drawers under the counter contained staples such as coffee, flour, oatmeal and sugar and had been supplied in bulk from large wooden barrels. The only meat available would be smoked ring bologna and summer sausage, since these did not need refrigeration. Good sandwiches could be made with sliced meat, cheese and Taystee bread.

The hardware and other necessary non-food items were located around and on the counter on the left side of the store looking from the front door. Here was the stock of work clothes, shoes, boots, overshoes, straw hats and all sorts of "work" clothing, but nothing one would wear to church.

They sold salt, both shaker and 50 pound blocks of salt for the cattle. They sold thread, needles and measuring tape, but no yard goods. One had to buy calico yard goods elsewhere for sewing. Before the days of electricity, it was so convenient that the Dell store always had kerosene and lamp repairs for the many homes then lighted with burning lamps.

They sold many horse collars in various sizes and various halters and leather repairs for horse harness. Valdy might be needed to locate or unpack a requested item. There were paint cans on the shelves on the wall behind the left counter. Pitch forks, manure forks, axes, shovels, rakes, were stacked against the wall. Many hand tools were available, but perhaps not in sight; you might need to ask Valdy or Thoralf to locate it within the dense accumulation of the always available large inventory at the Dell Store.

Fireworks were available for celebration before July 4th. Old timers claimed that the Schankes had the biggest fireworks supplies available in the area.

In the far left corner of the store was the door to the Shankes' private living quarters. Connie Mosby, the Pastor's daughter, remembers that during the 1950's a calendar picture of the Dionne quintuplets hung for several years on that door. She also remembered the usual large stalk of bananas hanging from the ceiling in the opposite back corner on the food side of the store.

Just outside the door at the back of the store was a platform used for loading and receiving freight, especially the many barrels containing food products. Available during the fall and winter months, outside in 'cold-storage', would be a barrel or two containing slabs of lutefisk soaking in salt water brine.

Although the inventory available for sale was extensive, it would be unimportant compared to the unique personalities of Thoralf and Waldemar. If this would be described in "show business" terms, Thoralf would be the dependable "straight" actor and Valdy the "comic". But these unique humble Norwegian men were not actors, they were natural salesmen who enjoyed every day that they would meet, delight and serve each customer.

Thoralf, the administrator of everything serious at the store, was the older brother having been born in 1886; Waldemar, born in 1896, was always the entertainer with the whole world as his stage. He could sell, explain and answer questions whenever he was not innovating some fun for the customer with his extraordinary imagination. Real Norwegians may use "W's and "V's' interchangeably so he could be called either "Valdy' or "Waldy".

In later years, Thoralf was the person to see if you wanted to buy farm machinery, tires, binder twine, rope or place an order for farm seeds, garden seeds or livestock feed. It was mostly Thoralf, who was in charge of the shed west of the store where these things were stored. This building had been added during the 1910-1920 decade and it stored these larger items and also was used to store the wool and hides that Thoralf purchased from the farmers. He was well known for paying the very best prices and was known to be the largest buyer in the county of wool and hides. This included hides of farm animals, mink, muskrat, beaver, skunk, jack rabbit, and cottontail rabbit. Some recall an offensive skunk odor permeating the area, even within the store, depending on the wind direction.

Melvin Bromeland was the young lad in the community who was perhaps most like Mark Twain's character, Huckleberry Finn, because Thoralf hired him to be the "hide-skinner" on a "per-pelt" basis for all the dead animals brought to the store that had been purchased from farmers and trappers.

Melvin had a simple idea that eliminated the skunk smell at the store. His solution was to take the carcass to the farm cow-yard next door and bury the carcass in the manure pile for several days. After washing it clean in the river, the problem was solved and Melvin could produce another pelt. He saved and was able to purchase his first bicycle with his earnings as a hide-skinner.

Pastor Mosby and his family lived across the street from the store and the Mosby daughter, Connie, recalled some of the memorable tales that have survived to be here included. Connie was a precocious child, who spent spare-time hours enjoying and being enjoyed by Valdy and Thoralf, perhaps often on a daily basis in the summer time.

The following is recollection, perhaps written in 1972 by Connie Mosby (later Larson), of her times spent with the Schanke brothers:

"I just wonder how many bottles of pop I drank while sitting on a nail keg talking to Valdy. It's unbelievable how many things were in that store and even more amazing how quickly the men could find things when they were needed.

Looking more deeply, the store would never have been what it really was, had it not been for the two that owned it, Valdy and Thoralf. What charming personalities they had and what a pest I was at times. I think they gave me a piece of candy or a slice of meat just to get rid of me.

I remember I would trail Thoralf out to that shed where he kept his skins where I would pester him with questions. I never learned too much about trapping, but I surely did a lot of talking. I wonder if my mom remembers the evenings we would be at home and would hear Thoralf playing the organ. It wasn't very often, but he really did play it.

Then there was Valdy. I really bothered him, but I think he loved it. He used to tell of many things that happened around Dell before I was born. I was usually sitting on a nail keg drinking some more pop.

But when I think of him, I remember the songs he would sing and the ones he taught me. Did you ever hear him sing, "A Preacher Went A Hunting" or "Tit Willow"? I have a favorite and I wish I could be there to sing it for you. It sounds much better with a melody, but it goes like this:

> *Just as I got down the pike,*
> *the horse began to balk;*
> *I felt just like a galk,*
> *so mad I couldn't talk.*
> *All the lads along the line*
> *began to yell and squawk—*
> *Hey Bill, Say Bill,*
> *You better get off and walk.*

There were the evenings that the farmers would gather at the Dell Store and discuss their day in the fields. That is, the farmers and Connie Mosby. I wasn't included in their conversation, but someone usually bought me another bottle of pop.

I've just touched on a few things that I remember. There's so much more. When I'm alone, I like to think about the place where I grew up and I wouldn't trade it with anyone else. The Schanke brothers were an important part of my life. I was the "pest". Just maybe I added a little bit to their lives when we lived there.

> *Connie Mosby Larson*
> *1812 Third Avenue N.W.*
> *Waverly, Iowa"*

It was fun to hear the "preacher stories" told about the times he came to the store and found a surprise, often on the preacher and sometimes on those in the store doing what a few loitering farmers might try.

Just after dark one evening, Thoralf announced to the gathered farmers near the pot-bellied stove, that he had just received a shipment of beautiful oysters and asked, *"Would you guys like to see some really big oysters?"* There was a quick unanimous declaration that *"WE"* should have an oyster supper. Except for one problem, without refrigeration in the store, there was no milk to make oyster stew.

That problem was also solved quite quickly, *"Well, we can steal some milk from the preacher's cow in the cow yard behind the parsonage across the road. I'll go milk the preacher's cow,"* volunteered one of the farmers.

With the stolen milk, Thoralf prepared a tasty oyster stew. But while the stew was being prepared in the Schanke brothers' living quarters in the next room, a guilty conscience settled upon several of the men which might require a confession. *"After all, this was the preacher's cow"*, they commiserated, *"and we had stolen the milk."*

So they telephoned Preacher Mosby and invited him to the store to join them for an oyster stew that evening, accompanied by a proper confession.

Most people never realized, nor was it widely known, that in that innocent little Dell Store, a bit of poker, including gambling with real coins, actually occurred on occasion even during daylight hours. Since there was no table on which to play cards and only nail kegs, pails, and barrels for seats in the back of the store, there remained only one place to accommodate a bit of poker.

This was the narrow only uncluttered counter surface area about two foot wide between the brown paper roll dispenser and the coffee grinder where all the store sales were conducted and payment properly afforded. Under the counter on the back side of the counter, available only to Valdy and Thoralf, were several large drawers each containing bulk grocery staples supplied from the large wooden barrels such as sugar, flour, and oatmeal sold by weight in a brown paper sack.

So two men would stand on each side of the narrow bare counter area to play a bit of "stud poker". During times preceding World War II, it was not acceptable among certain pietistical Lutherans to use regular playing cards for any purpose, especially gambling. Those were the days when families in their parlor games would instead use "Rook cards" which were actually quite similar to regular playing cards, but without the "royalty" on the larger valued cards.

On this day, the game was progressing well and one of the men happened to glance out the east window by the front door to see the pastor walking briskly toward the store. Quickly, the fellows behind the counter, opened the sugar drawer and with one arm movement swished the forbidden cards down into the opened sugar drawer.

As the pastor walked in, they all faked innocence and stood with hands at their sides while one of the Schankes asked, *"Well hello, Pastor. What can we do for you today?"* His response came smoothly and quickly, *"I want to buy some sugar, OUT OF THAT DRAWER."* as he pointed over the counter at what he knew to be the drawer for bulk sugar. I was never told what happened next, so I can only imagine the laughter and conversation that followed. "Score one" for Pastor Mosby.

When I was a fourth grader in District 97, a one-room school, my teacher (of German descent) opened the day on a Monday morning by telling the dozen or more students of all 8 grades about her unique experience of going to the Dell Store the past Saturday. The location of my school was north of our farm and just a bit north of area of Norwegians who regularly frequented the Dell Store. I was the only student who wasn't totally of German descent and I was perhaps the only student in the school who had often been to the Dell Store. Our farm happened to be on the "dividing line" between the Norwegians who had settled south of our farm and the Germans who settled north of our farm.

Mrs. Stallkamp began by telling us that she had heard so much about the uniqueness of the Dell Store, so she and her husband decided to go to see what her friends had told her about the store that *"had everything"*. They really had no intention to buy anything that day, so when she entered and was asked, she decided to buy a Hershey candy bar although she didn't see that label on any candy that was on display on the counter with the food and candy display. She saw large jars with hard candy and the hard candy on a stick called, "suckers", so she asked Valdy for a Hershey candy bar. Valdy said, *"Ya sure, we got a whole new box of Hersheys just the other day."*

Valdy walked over to the left side of the store where the hardware, shoes and work clothes were displayed. He picked up two new horse collars that had just been delivered for their inventory. After he lifted the horse collars, he found the newly delivered box of Hershey candy bars. He opened the box and sold my delighted teacher one Hershey candy bar, who now could tell us of her first experience at the Dell Store. As she spoke, I smiled, because I had been to that store many times. I already knew so many things about that store.

Perhaps the oldest story about the comedian, Valdy, was told to me by my father who had seen Valdy entertain in some sort of a gathering in the basement dining hall at the Dell Church. Valdy had been asked to tell a story to entertain the group. My father has no recollection of the actual story that he told. My father only remembered how Valdy told the story that kept the entire group laughing constantly as he spoke.

Valdy wore a mask to tell the story. The only unique part of the mask was the right eye which had an exaggerated eye-lid that was controlled by pulling a string to cause that large eye to close upon pulling the string. Doesn't sound very funny yet does it? But at the end of each sentence, Valdy would pause, and as he took a really deep breath, he would pull the string to close his right eye before continuing to talk when the eye was opened and his lungs filled for another sentence. It didn't take very many sentences and deep breaths as the big eye performed for the room before it was filled with healthy laughter. It surely wasn't necessary to remember the actual story line that he told so successfully that evening for one to retain a lasting memory. I can only suspect that it might have been a rhyming ditty similar to the nonsensical songs he loved to sing for the entertainment of persons like his very close buddy, Connie Mosby.

When I was old enough to have my own "bundle-team" of horses to haul oats bundles to the threshing machine, it was always customary to buy a new straw hat to begin the threshing season. It was the most fun of the summer for the neighbors to work together in this cooperative and social neighborhood gathering at all the farms in the neighborhood.

My best friend, Duffy, and I would go to the Dell Store to purchase our annual new straw hat for the threshing season. I remember Duffy and me standing near the counter on the left side of the store where the clothing and hardware was displayed. The counter had a pile of straw hats, because this was the season that all the farmers wore straw hats. This year there happened to be a new innovation in straw hats that I had never before seen. Valdy fitted each of us with a hat which had a green plastic visor in the front brim of the hat. I was not too sure I wanted to try something so new and different. Just then Valdy spoke up and like the true salesman he was, complimented us with our fancy straw hats by saying, *"Oh my, that's the latest 'stale from Paree."* It was typical creative nonsense from Valdy, intended to entertain. We smiled at his thought, but neither of us was daring enough to wear hats with the green front visor, because we weren't sure the plastic would stand up to the wear and tear for a year of protecting our ears and eyes from the sun.

Rene and I moved to our farm in 1954 and used the Dell store often. The first thing that brought us to the store was my wife's conclusion that if she was going to be a farmer's wife, she would not want to wear her diamond wedding rings when in the garden and doing other chores outside of the house. She wanted to buy a plain gold wedding band to occasionally replace her diamond wedding rings. I knew about the wholesale catalogs that Thoralf had shown to me. We not only bought the gold band for her, but a few years later, I bought a really wide men's gold wedding band that I yet wear after all these years, all from Thoralf's wholesale catalog at whole-sale prices.

By this time Thoralf was selling farm trailers and some oth-er farm machinery, all available behind the store. Thoralf had been selling a short-line of farm machinery, and could supply the "Su-per-Six front-end loader" that I needed for my farm tractor. I had seen that loader previously and had researched it and it was avail-able at the Dell store. I used it for many years for moving snow and cleaning hog barns. All from the full-service Dell Store.

By now our family was expanding with two young children. We needed some bedroom furniture, and again the wholesale cata-log at the Dell Store was the affordable answer. We bought two sets of excellent quality maple hardwood bedroom sets. The drawers were all assembled dove-tailed at the corners and although we have now down-sized our furniture needs, we still enjoy the quality furniture that was purchased at the Dell Store 60 years ago.

Prior to World War II Dell Store sold shotguns, rifles and ammunition. It has been claimed that the first fox-hunt in the state was organized at the Dell Store. Perhaps this idea was originated by the "boys" in the back of the Dell Store. By word-of-mouth the foxhunters would meet in front of the store on a Sunday afternoon at 2:00 PM. I suspect that perhaps it occurred after the boys in the back of the store had heard that fox had been sighted in a certain neighborhood.

A Dell Store fox-hunt required a minimum of 12 hunters with shotguns, but perhaps 16 hunters would be more advisable. Most all the roads in the county had intersections every mile making a checkerboard of squares of farm land, one mile on each side, each containing 640 acres. Three or four hunters would line up along each side of the one-mile square. The set time to begin the hunt was announced at the store when the men gathered for the hunt. The hunters would all line up along the 4 miles around the square to all begin to walk toward the center of the square at the preannounced time.

I know, I know, you are thinking right now of the extreme disadvantage imagined of the results of a 'circular firing squad'. Do not worry because the group does not walk very far toward the center of the square before a frightened fox is sighted and the hunt quickly ends. Remember that a shotgun's pellets really do not travel very far when you consider the guy on the other side is a mile away. Apparently a fox early notices the movement of a hunter and attempts to escape, but comes into the sights of a gun at every possible route of escape.

Really, all the fox-hunts I attended were actually a bit boring. We walked a very short distance and the hunt was completed in a very few minutes at the sound of a fired shotgun. For some reason only one fox was harvested in each hunt that I was a participant.

Hunters never got within shooting range of the guy on the opposite side of the field. The Dell Store invented, advertised and executed fox hunts for a bit of fun on a sunny autumn or spring afternoon when there were no crops in the fields.

Both Valdy and Thoralf were well educated and well read. It was claimed by some that Thoralf was the smartest man in the area. He had memorized much of the Bible and the U.S. Constitution and had opinions about each. His special opinion was about biblical prophecy, and rumor has it that his opinion and the Pastor's opinion resulted in an unresolved disagreement.

Thoralf was an accomplished violinist and played the piano and (foot-pumped) reed organ which is now on display at the Faribault County Historical Society.

Valdy had been a student at the Chicago Conservatory of Music. Thoralf was known to sing in a quartet at church. Each of the men regularly attended Sunday worship and always sat in the balcony at the rear of the church. From there they could exit quickly to get to the store to provide a service for those who might need to make a purchase after church. But Valdy would smile and proclaim, *"Hurry please, Sunday's a day of rest, ya know."* Actually the store would close after the worshippers completed their purchase of perhaps some bulk ice cream, a loaf of bread or some cold meat and cheese for their "day of rest".

A constant occupant of the store was Valdy's cat who was regularly found soaking up the warmth of the pot-bellied stove in the rear of the store. I wish my friend, Duffy, were still here to once again tell me the name of Valdy's cat. Every time he repeated the name, I laughed. I can only describe the name as a complicated collection of consonants and vowels with a Norwegian accent that most people could not repeat or pronounce. It was simply funny. It was another unique creation of Valdy's humor; however, it is my belief that no person is now living who might be able to repeat that famous cat's name.

There is a terrible rumor, which is actually not likely to be true, that Valdy's cat delivered her litter of kittens in the partially filled barrel of oatmeal. Because of an illicit story which quickly spread in this homogenous community, perhaps the sale of oatmeal steeply fell off for a time at the Dell Store.

It was a simple fact and not a rumor that the barrel that Valdy's cat used daily for sleeping was often shared together with Paul Anderson's dog. Obviously, the usual dog-cat animosity between them had long since been reconciled because of their simple, but ample, diplomacy. Even the animals were happy at Dell Store.

Valdy loved children and children loved all the jars of penny candy sitting on the counter top near the door. Valdy's humor would shine when he participated with the children. If a child would say, *"I'll take 3 cents worth of that candy"*. As the child would point, Valdy would answer gruffly, *"You take anything here and you'll be arrested"*. The store sold Hershey candy bars for one cent that fit nicely on a graham cracker.

Small children loved it when Valdy lovingly claimed a small child to be *"Valdy's Lil' Thoosla One"*. He had many entertaining little song "ditties" that he would sing to them like:

> *Preacher went a-hunting,*
> *T'was on a Sunday morn.*
> *Tho' it was against his religion,*
> *He took his gun along.*
> *He shot himself a quail,*
> *And a great big grizzly bear.*

Older kids would always prefer to buy their pop to drink at the Dell store for 7 cents a bottle because the hardware store and the Farmer's Elevator charged 10 cents a bottle at Frost, three miles south of Dell. There had been a time when pop at Dell Store sold for 5 cents.

On the last day of mid-summer Bible School at the church, the children all were invited to come across the road to the Dell Store for free candy.

Valdy could also think of ways to have fun with the adults who came. One of the funniest was Valdy seriously asking Ernie Fenske, who always was dressed a bit uniquely casual and different, *"Did your folks have any children?"* I was never told what happened next.

Valdy had a number of favorite sayings that were repeated from time-to-time:

"If you want to pinch anything, pinch the coconuts."

"Now you can't clack me."

"Scuse me, my phone." (many years before cell phones)

But the best retort that often came from this lovely man and always caused a smile, happened as he received money from a customer and turned to punch the keys on the noisy cash register; he in pure self-depreciating gentle humor spoke slowly with a Norwegian accent and said,

"It vasn't worth it, but ve NEED the mon-nee."

Chapter Seven

We Were Treated
Like Royalty

My wife, Irene (Rene) often told of her childhood memories at Trinity Lutheran Church in Blue Earth, MN where her mother, Anna Skogerboe Chrisianson served as organist for 35 years.

Anna Christianson at Trinity Lutheran Church organ.

Rene's early memories of worshipping every Sunday were sitting with her father, Otto Conrad Christianson and her seven siblings every Sunday morning. Otto and his family nearly filled the entire

77

pew, while Anna served at the organ in the front of the church. The siblings were seated with the youngest child seated closest to Otto and the other siblings each seated next consecutively by increasing age. The eight children and their year of birth are: Dorothy Marie, 1920; Orlo John, 1922; Christopher Jay, (originally christened, Carol Jean)1924; LaVern Myrle, 1926; Irene (Rene) Lucille, 1928, twins-Janice Opal and Joyce Lee, 1930; and Esther Muriel, 1932.

Rene specifically remembers that there could be "consequences" when they returned home if any of them did not sit quietly and behave properly. At that age, her feet did not reach the floor as she sat, but she knew that it was not considered an infraction of behavior if she would swing her legs. She remembers that members of the congregation often complimented them on the family's good behavior.

The usual Sunday noon meal after church included a beef roast, which had been baking in the oven during church services. The family always walked the five blocks (almost a mile) to church. Anna needed time after the service to store her music and robe, while Otto and the children would leave promptly after the service. Otto would peel the potatoes for boiling and set the table by the time Anna arrived for their usual mashed potatoes and roast beef dinner.

All of the members of the church can easily remember the cameo view of Anna at the organ wearing a serene, smiling contenance and her braided hair circling the top of her head, as she used all of her appendages at the organ.

Anna was the sole organist for the church for most of the years that she served Trinity as organist. The pastor's wife, Inga Thompson, would substitute for her in emergencies or if she had a conflict. Anna received a yearly salary of $400, plus whatever she received for funerals and weddings. Anna bought and donated to the church music library, the organ sheet music that she needed from time to time. Her favorite music included the melodious pieces composed by Johann Sebastian Bach and all the memorable Christmas music that made those holiday services so special.

Irene had fond memories of hearing her mother on the piano, softly playing Christian hymns late in the evenings after the children were in their beds, while she awaited Otto's occasional late return from his job.

Otto had been employed by Schwen's Ice Cream Company to make regular deliveries to grocery stores, pharmacies, restaurants, bars and service stations mostly in southern Minnesota and northern Iowa. He died in an accident on an extremely icy road on December 29, 1942, as he returned from deliveries at Forest City, Iowa. He was unable to avoid striking a semi-trailer truck that jack-knifed ahead of him on the slippery highway. This left Anna to support and care for eight active children aged 10 to 22 at the time.

Otto Christianson with his Schwen's Ice Cream Truck, October 1942.

Without Otto's income, finances were extremely limited for the active family of 9. In addition to her organ playing at church, Anna's main source of income was their rental of the "Green Gable Cabins", five of which were located on their extra lot just east of their back door. Otto started this enterprise several years before his death as a sideline source of income that would involve the labors of the entire family. The children helped Anna change the bedding, clean the cabins and *iron* the sheets for the rentals. The "Green Gable" franchise of the rental of unheated cabins began during the Great Depression and preceded the modern motels of today.

Several years after Otto's death, Anna converted the large garden spot on an extra lot on the west side of the house into camp sites with electrical hook-ups for travel trailers and small mobile homes. This became the first motor home park in the area at the time.

Rene and I left Caledona, MN in 1954, where I had served as an extension soils agent for the University of Minnesota, to begin our farming enterprise on the farm that my grandfather, Ole Johnson, had built. We now would be living next door to my parents' farm which was located six miles east of Blue Earth, MN. We had been existing on a salary of $300 a month during the four-year employment by the U. of M. College of Agriculture, Forestry and Home Economics, beginning after my graduation from there.

That we had excessive dreams and meager assets to begin this new farm venture would be an obvious conclusion. Beside our good intentions, our total assets included $300 in savings, a 1952 Pontiac sedan automobile, and a 1942 Chevrolet pick-up truck that I had recently purchased from the U.S. Conservation Service for $300. The soybean seed that I needed for my first crop was generously donated from the soybeans harvested from my father's previous crop. He also made a gift of five purebred Hereford heifers and three pregnant sows to start the livestock part of my expected enterprise.

Rene and I ordered 500 female Leghorn chicks, which we would feed through the summer and fall, before we could begin to sell eggs, which we would need to pay for the food on our table. The three sows had litters that summer that were disappointingly less than average. My hope of producing an 'extensive' hog herd quickly would now take longer than I had hoped.

My parents were generous and happy to have us back on the farm living close by. Their rental offer included the joint use of my father's farm machinery, while we worked together on both farms. My land rental obligation was an unwritten simple 50/50 share-crop lease. This meant that in eighteen months, I would enjoy my first crop income which would be half of the soybean and corn crops harvested; the other half of the harvest would satisfy my rent obligation to my parents. To make the short-term financial outlook seem even more bleak, I planned to feed the corn harvested to my livestock.

Now as I think of it, I must have been really eager to farm. We must have simply ignored the reality of scant income for a long period of time. We had accepted the fact that increased cash flow from farm production would be in the distant future. Whether we knew it or not, it really was a "steep hill to climb".

We both had college degrees and for three years, Rene had taught in the Brownsville grade school, located five miles from our Caledonia home. Looking from the school playground, which was only blocks from the shore of the Mississippi River, she could often get a close-up view of tugboats pushing long strings of river barges, because all river traffic passing the town of Brownsville is permanently routed to that side of the river.

Shortly after we moved in the spring of 1954, Rene acquired a teaching position, beginning that fall at the grade school at Delavan, MN, which was 6 miles from our farm. Income from her teaching contract greatly helped to solve our immediate cash flow problem, but accepting the job created a second problem. We would need someone to care for our two babies while Rene was at school; Pamela was now two years old and Dana was born in June, only two months before her teaching duties would begin.

Rene asked her mother, Anna, if she would like to undertake that responsibility. By that time, all of the Christianson children were out of the home and on their own. We both had agreed that she would be the best person in the world to care for our children. Her loving care would be priceless.

The Christianson Green Gable Cabins. (Irene and Dorothy in doorway.)

Without words, "Grandma Ann's" smile at that request revealed her answer even before she spoke. Twenty years previous, the Green Gable Cabins produced reliable income, but no longer, because motels had become available and popular. Anna now had to make a decision as to her future use of the large family home and business that had so many memories and had well served her family during both good and difficult times.

For the first year of her enhanced grandmother duties with us, she lived at our home during the weekdays and would return home for the weekends to serve as organist at church and to tend the cabins, if she had a renter, but usually she had no renters.

She listed the house for sale with a realtor soon after she began her responsibilities at our home. She knew the big house was more than she needed or could afford. The former rental income had now become almost nonexistent. After she announced that she had listed her property with a realtor, we asked what her intentions were after her house would be sold. She answered that she would look for a small house that would meet her needs.

The Christianson family house sold after a short time. Anna disposed of most of her household property and moved into the bedroom in our home that she had previously been using during the weekdays.

Anna never again mentioned the subject of her stated intention to buy a smaller home, nor did Rene or I ever ask about it. Grandma Ann became so comfortable as a special part of our family, that the "small house" subject was never mentioned again. Her presence had become such a mutual blessing, that it would have been a heartfelt loss to our family had she left us to live in that "small house".

I will always remember and greatly appreciate the time she gently scolded her daughter as she said, *"You really should be nicer to Vic, because he's so good to you."* Does a mother-in-law ever get any better than that? Not a chance!

Unlike the popular often-told mother-in-law stories, our "Grandma Ann" was my "angel mother-in-law". Everyone in our family loved her loving care, which in addition to caring for our babies, might include a baked roast beef dinner, even on days when it wasn't yet Sunday. Without being asked, she had quietly mastered and assumed the complete control of the kitchen, especially the oven. We were treated like royalty.

She lived with us and was an intimate part of our family for eighteen years. During those years, our home became the "hub" of her extended family, particularly her grandchildren who often spent weeks during the summer months living at our farm. Grandma Ann loved to have them come.

The size of our family was often increased substantially with "cousins from the city", who would gravitate to what they all called "the farm" in the summer months for weeks at a time. I personally told Grandma Ann, *"Let them come. Together, we'll feed them. I'll provide the groceries. We can just set more plates at the table for them".*

In the evening her rocking chair would be filled with a smiling Grandma Ann and the youngest cousin in her arms, who was now relaxing at the end of an active day with the collie dogs and the horse named Shoney, who loved children. The huge lawn was a place where cousins could run and play games.

Whenever the subject of cousins at the farm is discussed, the first memories recalled are the days that the cousins as a group daily "organized" in the playhouse that had formerly been a brooder house to start baby chicks.

One time about a half dozen cousins organized and worked diligently together during the entire day preparing everything that they could think of that they might ever possibly need during the night for the group to sleep outside together in the playhouse. It was a much anticipated event. After the evening meal, they all quickly departed to the playhouse.

Unfortunately, early in the dark evening as they were settling into their agreed personal spots for the night, Chuck, the oldest boy, began to tell ghost stories. One by one, beginning with the youngest cousin, they all left the playhouse. Each came in to tell a different unique reason he or she could no longer remain outside. The one creative reason that I recall which was used by one of the tots was, *"I think it might rain"*.

The last to come in was Chuck, who simply explained that he wasn't going to stay out there in the dark alone. It seems that he may have "cooked his own goose".

Each summer culminated with a reunion of Grandma Ann's family. This included the parents and all the cousins who could come on a weekend late in the warm months. Somehow 30-45 people found places to sleep in our 5 bedroom home.

The problem of baths and the warm water supply to bathe the many cousins on Saturday evening was solved by renting the municipal swimming pool at Bricelyn, MN for a time after the pool had closed to the public. The cousins loved this idea that solved our problems. The pool showers provided the baths and after all the activity, they were all so tuckered out that "time for bed" was an easy sell.

The cousins, now adults, have often expressed the joy they experienced at the farm as a child. Much of this is a tribute to Grandma Ann, who shaped and created a generation of grandchildren whose lives were blessed by the traits that to her came so naturally as she treated us all like royalty.

These fond recollections have resulted in multiple, subsequent, similar reunions hosted by Cyndi Rafferty at her large home in Sandwich, IL. Cyndi was one of the cousins who frequently enjoyed Grandma Ann's lap in the rocking chair at the end of an active day at the farm. In my biased opinion, Cyndi has inherited nearly all of the wonderful, caring, selfless attributes reflected by Grandma Ann. Her well-appointed and landscaped large home with a swimming pool and her generous efforts to host the group in the same manner that it happened at the farm, have always made it a great success.

As I write this, the invitation is out and it will happen again on June 30 to July 2, 2017. Cyndi carries on in her always loving manner because she learned well from the one who quietly treated all of us like royalty.

It was toward the end of Anna's 35 years at the church organ that she felt she needed to practice to be prepared for Sunday morning services. During her earlier years of rearing her own family, she **never** had time to practice for Sunday services except at the time of choir practice each Wednesday evening with the choir. She must have felt that she now needed practice, because she began coming to Blue Earth shortly after noon with Rene, who came to shop for groceries. This was at a time after Rene had discontinued teaching. Anna would remain at the church to practice while Rene returned home after shopping. After practicing at the organ, Anna would walk several blocks to my law office to accompany me home at 5:00 pm.

On a late fall afternoon about 4 or 5 inches of snow had fallen on the highway during the day. After my office had closed for the day, Anna and I began the six-mile drive home. The road was yet unplowed that mild afternoon, leaving two wheel tracks in each lane where vehicles had previously traveled in the snow. I was driving 45 mph when I should have been driving 35 mph. We slowly headed toward the easy slope of the ditch. The car was out of control at that speed in the slippery snow. The car coasted along in the bottom of the ditch as the speed dissipated and I realized that I had control again. I simply accelerated a bit to get enough momentum to drive up out of the slight ditch embankment and onto the highway to continue toward home at a more reasonable speed.

During the entire episode, Grandma Ann peacefully sat next to me wearing her 3-button rubber overshoes, while all of the time holding her hands on the top of her purse. This happened before the days of seat belts. She did not say a word until we were safely back on the highway, when she softly said, *"My, I'm glad you were driving and not me."* I thought, but my ego would not allow me to say, *"If you had been driving , it would not have happened."*

Later in her life, Anna's organ playing abilities were not up to the expected quality the choir members had experienced for those 35 years. The choir director at the time, Marne Aleckson, agonized over how to inform Anna that she should discontinue serving as organist every Sunday. All the musicians had noticed the difference, but no one could bring themselves to say anything. For those many years, Inga Thompson, the pastor's wife, had been the only substitute available. However, now there were a number of younger, talented organists available.

The group decided on a plan and Marne became the appointed one to break the news to Anna that she should be relieved as organist after her years of faithful service. Marne claims it was one of the hardest things she had ever been required to do.

Marne finally met Anna and asked if it would be all right if the other organists would serve four Sundays each month and Anna could be organist on each month that had a fifth Sunday, Also Anna would have any weddings or funerals when she was requested. After a deep breath, Marne was greatly relieved when Anna responded, *"Oh, I think that would be wonderful."*

Thus ended a much appreciated era of her musical service at Trinity Lutheran Church. Anna's grace and love never ended. The simple humble response of acceptance given to Marne that day was once again done in a royal manner of grace. She could do no less.

Chapter Eight

The Sister Reunion

My mother-in-law, "Grandma Ann", (Anna Christianson) as our family called her, had become an irreplaceable beloved member of our household, which lasted 18 years until her death.

It all started when she sold her large family home in Blue Earth, MN. I had invited her to make her home with us *"until she would find a smaller house"* which she had mentioned was her original intention. Our entire family, without exception, found that she was easy to love as she lavished all of us with her love, which consisted partially of feeding and caring royally for us in the absence of Rene, who was off to school doing her teaching duties.

She must have enjoyed being a part of our family, because she never bothered looking for that smaller house. We never mentioned it again. There existed a comfortable mutual feeling that she was an integral part of our family. She recognized and knew that she was not just a maid and baby sitter, but rather she belonged to our family with all the privileges that status afforded.

It was mid-summer that year when she found out that her sisters, Nora Puzina and Sally (Selma) Thompson, would be coming from California to visit her and her other relatives here in the Midwest. After discussion with Rene and me, she decided to invite all the "sisters" to spend a few days together here at our farm home.

As I recall, Nora and Sally were going to be with us for a week. So Grandma Ann invited her other sister, Melinda Otis, and her sister-in-law, Norma Skogerboe, to come and spend as much time at the farm as they wished for a sister reunion. There were 5 bedrooms at our home and our 4 children would willingly sacrifice their beds in exchange for sleeping bags for a few days. I'm sure the sisters had slept together in double beds in their past lives as children and happily adjusted easily to this condition once again for a few days.

Once the four arrived, most of the time was spent in the family room together around the dining room table with coffee, talking over the past as well as those stories in their lives that needed to be updated to the group. Although I spent little time with them, I can only imagine the distinct and unique personalities involved which might cause a bit of sibling interaction between these five ladies.

Melinda and Grandma Ann seemed to be the most alike, being reserved with a constant smile and always displaying proper attitudes and presentations. These two could accommodate any situation that might arise with aplomb and acceptance, even when it might turn out to be a bit uncomfortable. Likewise, they would both laugh heartily at any anecdote, particularly if it were at their own expense.

Sister-in-law, Norma, fit into this same comfortable description except Norma could also be a storyteller and had a way of letting her creative imagination carry the group in a different direction occasionally. To me the word, "pixie", seemed to describe her comfortable personality.

Sister Nora's character is the most difficult to explain. According to the stories told me about her past, she was acclaimed to be the renegade of the family. Seems like every family has one sibling that wants to march by a different drummer than the rest of the family. Nora was opinionated and a bit outspoken with a tinge of trying to be the oldest and in control, although actually it was Grandma Ann who was the eldest sister.

Last, and the youngest of the group, was the delightful, energetic Sally. She seemed always upbeat and laughing. Her problem in a setting like this was her inability to ever completely tell a funny story or joke; she often tried. She would destroy the story by giggling so hard just before the punch line that it was seldom that she would complete her story to the end.

The sister reunion was going charmingly and the ladies seemed to be having a great time recalling old times, telling forgotten happenings, and doing the things we all like to do at a good reunion. The smiling conversation seemed to circle freely all around the dining room table or at least that was what it seemed to me that morning when I left to paint one of the farm buildings outside.

I had built a scaffolding which amounted to a couple planks supported about 40 inches off the ground running along the full 42 feet of the east side of the single story building. I needed this scaffolding so that I could reach the top part of the wall which was about 10 feet in height.

My silence up there on the scaffolding in the sunshine with my paintbrush in hand was interrupted by Sally who came out in a huff. *"Give me a paint brush. I need to work. I like to work, always did. Gotta get out of that house. I can't put up with them bossing me around any longer! They think they can do it just like they did when we were kids."*

I don't really know who were the 'them' or the 'they' that she referred to, that had so upset Sally, but I had my suspicions. I always wondered what it was all about, but I never asked for an explanation; rather I obliged by handing her a paint brush, helped her up on the scaffolding and enjoyed her company. We completed the job much faster than I had expected. She said she had always been a tomboy and wasn't afraid of heights. Sally could never do wrong in my book.

The highlight of the reunion happened the next morning. Our large bathroom upstairs, near the bedrooms, had an 8-foot countertop with two sinks and two mirrors. The ladies all exclusively used this bathroom before retiring.

Norma (the pixie) was the last to retire that evening. On the far north end of the bathroom countertop was a glass half-filled with water in which was soaking a pair of false teeth. On the far south end of the bathroom counter was another glass half-filled with water with another pair of false teeth. Two of the sisters apparently had prepared for a night of sound sleep without the distraction of their teeth. The naughty sister-in-law, Norma, couldn't help herself. She switched only the uppers, putting the southerly upper teeth in the north glass and likewise the northerly upper teeth in the south glass. I can only imagine her gleefulness as she retired awaiting what might happen that next morning.

The next morning just before breakfast, Sally started complaining that for some silly reason her teeth didn't feel right. Then Nora chimed in that something seemed wrong with her teeth too.

"You don't suppose that I made a mistake and confused my teeth with yours and mixed them up, do you?" Sally asked.

All the ladies laughed and laughed until the tears came, as the two ladies held their upper false teeth under the faucet and exchanged so that their teeth felt comfortable again. Poor Sally laughed the loudest and the longest, since she was positive that it was she that made the mistake.

"Naughty Norma" laughed too, but never uttered a word of explanation. The story lived well beyond the lifetimes of Sally and Nora, who never knew the truth.

Three sisters - Sally Thompson, Anna Christianson, Nora Puzina.

Chapter Nine

Shoney Acted Like People

O ften we had listened to people tell their stories of trail-riding with saddle horses on mountain trails; Rene and I each had an unfulfilled desire to ride horses on a mountain trail. It happened once while visiting friends who lived near a horse ranch in the foothills of Colorado.

The ranch owner assigned a pair of beautiful bay horses for Rene and me to ride. We were told that these were once used as race horses, but had been retired after they reached an age that made them undesirable for racing. Needless to say, these two horses were alert, responsive and ready to go; although we were not experienced riders, yet we were both very comfortable on these well-trained horses.

Our previous experience of riding horses on vacation was once at Mackinac Island, where no vehicles except emergency vehicles are allowed and the only transportation available to vacationing visitors was the rental of either bicycles or horses. At that time the horses assigned to us were totally unresponsive to our efforts to make them run or even walk faster. They would only walk at the pace they chose and it wasn't fast or exciting. Actually, it was a very boring afternoon.

These responsive Colorado horses were totally unlike the horses we had experienced while on Mackinac Island. Unbeknownst to us at the time, riding a trail in the foot hills below the high mountains of Colorado would turn out to be a memorable day for additional reasons, other than the enjoyable ride in beautiful mountain scenery.

Rene was enamored with her horse. She had previously talked about adding riding horses on our farm; we had an adaptable barn and we could enjoy a hobby of caring for riding horses.

After the ride that day, she tried, emotionally and unsuccessfully, to prevail upon me to buy these two horses, since they were exactly what she had in mind and that we "needed" on our farm. I immediately envisioned the cost, not only for the purchase of the two animals, but I could only imagine the exorbitant cost I would incur to transport these horses to Minnesota.

I used the transportation cost as an excuse and told her that we could surely find nice riding horses in Minnesota and not have to incur the cost of any transportation. She accepted the logic and agreed at the time, but I knew that we would be getting a horse to ride soon after our return from Colorado.

I inquired and found a local horse-trader named, Bill Grese, who brought a saddle horse to try out. The horse had a handsome light tan color with large white spots and a black mane and tail. He was a quarter-horse gelding and his age was unknown. Any horse trader knows that when the raised edges on their teeth are lost from wear, the horse is considered to be smooth-mouthed and is at least ten years old.

Bill recommended that this horse was "well-broke" and had been used as a saddle horse in the stock yards at Sioux Falls, South Dakota. I remember paying Bill $300 for the horse, delivered, to our farm. Unbeknownst to us at the time we had just acquired a new member in our family.

He was understood to be Rene's riding horse, but I could feed, care for him, and ride him whenever I wanted to ride. It was a really good deal for her, and I had not expected otherwise. Rene had chosen the names of each of our children, so she naturally assumed the horse-naming responsibility. She named her horse Shoshoni because her horse was born in the west and Shoshoni was a western town with an Indian name. His name was used for a few months, but it was soon shortened and he acquired a nickname and was thereafter always called Shoney.

Our son Dana and daughter Pamela were both in grade school at the time. Rene was a kindergarten teacher in Blue Earth. On pet day at her kindergarten class, children were encouraged to bring a pet to show and tell on that day.

Spike Piper, the school bus driver, claimed that he had the best job in the world. He told that on pet day, one child brought a small goldfish bowl with her pet goldfish riding inside. In a slightly whining voice, the little tyke told Spike, *"Please drive slowly, because I don't want my goldfish to get carsick."*

Susie Hagedorn successfully begged her father to bring her Shetland pony named Queenie to kindergarten for pet day. Queenie had produced a colt that Susie had named, Princess, which came to school with Queenie that day.

Susie was so proud; some of the children had never before been able to pet a pony. Because Susie was happy and she loved her teacher, she told Rene that she wanted Rene to have Princess, and *"keep her forever"*.

We later paid Susie $35 and brought the little horse home in the rear seat of our old 1949 Chevy after removing the lower cushion.

When Princess was a couple years older, our children often rode Princess, with Rene or me on Shoney, on the short trail in the woods along the river on our farm, which we had named, the "circle". We didn't keep a record, but perhaps Dana and I rode the two horses on the circle more often than Rene and Pamela.

Dana teaches Princess to neck-rein.

Several years later Pamela, like her mother, wanted a horse to ride that would be her horse. She had decided that she was too old to ride a Shetland pony. Dana, who was younger, often rode Princess and had succeeded in training Princess to "neck-rein", which is quite unusual, because few Shetland Ponies become that well trained. Shetlands are well-known to be a bit stubborn and have a mind of their own.

Pamela named her horse, Honey. She was a pretty palomino with a flowing white mane and tail and was not as tall as Shoney. Now our family had three horses to ride on the trail.

We had a small white-fenced pasture in front of our home, but with three horses grazing, the horses soon needed more grass to satisfy them. I installed a temporary single-wire electric fence to give them more grazing area around the barn and other farm buildings. The fence had a gate, which was a simple plastic handle with a hook at the end of the wire. We could lay the wire on the ground and drive over it to go into the area of the farm buildings.

One day two farmers, Duffy and Harlan, had come to see me. We were standing near the barn talking together. Shoney quietly walked away from where he had been grazing and came to join our group. Shoney had come to complete a circle of four "guys" with his slightly lowered head so he could be at eye-to-eye level with the guys. He stood in the exact place a fourth farmer would have stood, if one were present. Perhaps he just wanted to be with the guys. It seemed that Shoney acted like people.

The horses were in the pasture by our house once, when Dana, who was perhaps 10 years old at the time, tried a trick that was foolish and a bit daring. As usual, Shoney was unrestrained without a halter and was comfortable with Dana walking near him in the area; he simply ignored Dana.

Shoney was grazing, when Dana walked up to Shoney's head until he straddled the horse's head and was on his neck. Shoney was surprised and simply raised his head too late to prevent the ordeal. Dana slid rearward on the horse's neck and then he turned around into riding position. This was a new trick that had never happened before and Shoney did not particularly care for the idea. The horse stood and did not move until Dana put pressure with his feet into Shoney's flank to make him begin to walk. The well-trained horse then responded as if he was being neck-reined when Dana leaned forward to touch Shoney's neck to turn him in various directions while walking around in the pasture. It was just a daring boy and a sensible horse without a bridle, halter or saddle.

Dana and Shoney in pasture.

Dana later told me that he was able to repeat that trick a number of times. Shoney always had an accommodating habit of lowering his head to allow us to put his riding bridle over his ears when we approached with his bridle in our hand. Dana said that he would walk up to him while sweet talking and petting him on his head and shoulders. When Shoney relaxed, Dana would place his hand on the top of his head and say, "Down, Shoney" and would repeat it again as often as necessary until his head was in grazing position and Dana would often be able to mount him in this unusual manner. Dana said Shoney was a wise-one with a mind of his own and sometimes he just didn't allow it. Dana tells me he mounted Shoney a number of times with sweet talk and petting.

I have to admit that during his youthful years, Dana often sweet talked his Dad into a privilege of some sort for himself, so I knew he could also be good at that effort with Shoney, who really had become a part of our family.

Often Rene would ask me to saddle Shoney for her, so she could ride Shoney on our trail that we called the circle. On the first half mile, she would be in the wooded area by the river following on a deer trail, where we all always rode at a walking pace. However, the last half-mile was in the wide road ditch along the highway by our farm. This final part of the circle was always ridden at a gallop. We would press Shoney in the flanks with our heels to bring him into a beautiful smooth canter. It was fun to end the ride with an invigorating sprint.

Once in late July, when the unmowed grass in the ditch was about 18 inches tall, Rene and Shoney were cantering toward home at a pleasant pace in this thick roadside ditch grass. Suddenly, Shoney felt something unusual against his front leg just above his hoof. It happened to be a half-mile length of smooth telephone wire hidden in the grass. Shoney was startled and reacted instantly. Still moving ahead at full speed, Shoney sprang abruptly to the right, away from the harmless wire, leaving Rene in midair without a horse. Rene thought Shoney may have suspected it to be rattlesnake, something that he may have previously experienced during his time in the west. She fell, her body still moving at the former speed as she hit the soft deep grass and rolled without any harm to herself.

After unseating a rider, most other horses would run toward home and stand at the barn door waiting to get in to relax. Not Shoney, who became concerned for Rene who lay in the grass. Just like a person, Shoney turned around, returned to Rene, and put his nose down to her body, as if checking the danger or her condition. It seemed as if he wanted to ask, *Are you OK?* Shoney stood still, Rene remounted and they both returned home.

Shoney and the cousins at reunion time.

Shoney and the cousins - Ellen Moreland and Matthew Johnson.

Often when the farmyard was full of children, we would place five or six of the young cousins on Shoney's back for a picture. They could sit anywhere on his back from his withers to his rear, he didn't mind. It is true that I had often said that the children could go between any two of Shoney's legs and he wouldn't pay any attention. It was never tried because all the children had a healthy respect and perhaps just a bit of fear for the big horse. Shoney knew when children were on his back, because he would act differently when a child was on his back than when an adult was riding him.

I had been gone for several weeks for group study in preparation for the Minnesota State Bar Exam. It was a perfect warm sunny July day when I returned to the farm and to my family for the weekend. It would be a relief and a refreshing time just to ride Shoney on the circle and just enjoy the peace and beauty with the woods, the river and the horse. I had an intention to have a relaxing ride as I slowly walked the horse through the quiet wooded scenery.

Matthew, who was three years old, wanted to ride with me. I had missed the family in my absence, so I put the child on the saddle in front of me. We walked the entire trail. It was so relaxing in the sunshine for both of us, that Matthew fell asleep as his head bobbed down toward his chest.

I believe Shoney knew the child was in the saddle, because in the road ditch, where we usually would sprint the rest of the way, Shoney just kept walking, which was totally unlike the usual routine for Shoney. Matthew was still asleep when I handed him off the saddle and down into his mother's arms. Just after that, I barely touched Shoney's flank and he immediatcly responded into a gallop across the yard. He understood that the child was no longer on his back.

One time he tried so hard to talk to us that it was laughable. The horses were in the white-fenced pasture in front of our house. Honey, Pamela's palomino mare, was pregnant and it was the next morning after the birth. I wouldn't have immediately noticed the horses when I walked out of the house that morning, but Shoney saw me first. He was very excited and came galloping toward me, and with his head across the fence, he looked directly at me and whinnied. When he knew that I saw him, he galloped back to the wobbly long-legged new foal trying to walk for the first time, lowered his head close to the foal, seeming to smell him, or maybe he was pointing to the little horse to tell me where to look.

Then at full speed, he galloped back and with his head over the fence whinnied again. He raced back the second time, circled the little foal and examined the foal again with his nose and raced back to tell me the third time as he stretched his head over the fence again and loudly explained the importance of that day's special event.

He was so proud. Perhaps he may have mistakingly thought he was responsible for the birth, but he actually told a story; he acted like people.

We enjoyed Shoney for a number of years, until his age began to show. It was at a time that our two younger boys, Matthew and Jayson, were in high school, while Pamela and Dana were at college. Our family had acquired a skiing vacation habit. We would ski in the Colorado or Wyoming mountains during the week following Christmas. On a Sunday afternoon on the return trip from skiing, we stopped at Shoshoni, Wyoming, for a noon lunch. Our family lunch topic came naturally. We told stories about our family horse who was also called Shoshoni.

During our vacation absence, our next-door neighbor, Wendell Erickson, was happy to care for our four horses, which were free to roam together in the large fenced barnyard. His only chore was to feed them hay and check the water supply.

Early Monday morning after our return home, he came to tell us a sad story, *"I'm so very sorry. I need to tell you, that Shoney died yesterday while you were gone. I really feel terrible that it happened while I was taking care of them."*

We assured him that we knew it was not his fault. He didn't cause the death and there would have been nothing he could have done to prevent the death.

Then Wendell told the rest of the story, *"It was really eerie. I have never seen anything like it. When I came to check on the horses yesterday morning, Shoney was so weak, that when he tried to stand up, his hind legs were unable to stand. Then something really weird happened. The other three horses came, nipped at his rear quarters and nudged him with their heads as if they were trying to help him stand up. He died shortly after that. I think that the other horses knew he was dying."*

Our family looked at each other knowingly. We all remembered that this drama in the barnyard happened on the morning that our family dined at Shoshoni, Wyoming.

I wonder if Shoney had taught all the other horses in the barnyard how to *"act like people"*.

Chapter Ten

Four "Wows" in the Holy Land

O ur family attended church nearly every Sunday morning at Immanuel Evangelical Church, three miles east of Blue Earth. Sunday school was always at 10 AM with the worship service following at 11 AM. Sunday school at Immanuel was not only for the youth. All ages studied a Bible lesson during the Sunday school hour on the Sabbath day. It was there that I confirmed my baptismal vows as a young lad. It was there that I was taught to pray and it was there that I heard all of those wonderful Bible stories told by diligent and inspired teachers and pastors.

I distinctly remember praying an unusual prayer at that time. I said, *"God, you know I've been taught that I must have faith. I have heard all of these stories of when Jesus walked the earth and some of them are kinda far-fetched and hard to believe. You know, God, if I could see the Holy Land and walk where Jesus walked, it would be a lot easier to believe those stories and have that faith that I need."*

After all these years, I still remember my talk to God at that time. My prayer given as a youth was truly answered when Rene and I visited the Holy Land in March, 1995. I actually walked on the very steps that Jesus used on his way to his final supper near the Garden of Gethsemane.

We had a wonderful ten-day conducted tour and stayed in 5-star hotels. Although our tour guide was a Jew, he knew his biblical history and was a very knowledgeable lecturer. The 45 people on the tour bus became a community as together we saw the sights that almost seemed familiar because we had heard the stories over the years. As I saw the places that were told about in those ancient Bible stories, a breath of life came into them, as I imagined the biblical characters being in the various locations in this actual land of the Bible.

Robert Schuller, the TV preacher, never uses bad words, but he does use the word "wow" for emphasis, explanation and amazement. That word appeared often, sometimes spoken, but always coming to my mind as we explored the Holy Land. I cannot help but use the word as I write and when I have told this story many times to others. There are four "wows" that I relive every time I review those days that I experienced the actual places where Christ once walked.

Wow #1

We had just been shown the place of the Last Supper. Unfortunately it is now the site of a small Moslem mosque. From there we could see the place a short distance away where Judas betrayed Christ and the place that the cock crowed. There was an ornamental cock on top of a mast to indicate the place where the cock did crow. Down the hill a bit further was the place where Judas had hung himself.

As we passed back toward our tour bus, only a few steps from the mosque, the tour guide mentioned, seemingly as an inconsequential few words that almost slipped his mind, that this is the only place existing today where we know for certain that Jesus actually walked. As he kept walking by, he simply pointed down toward the limestone stair-steps set into the hillside only a few feet from our path. I could see the Garden of Gethsemane a very short distance beyond the Kidron valley. Although I did not speak, huge ideas with an exclamation mark raced across my mind. I could not leave this spot and simply follow our group walking past this special place. *"Wow"*, the ideas came to me, *"God answered my prayer. These are the stair-steps that Jesus took when he walked from the Garden of Gethsemane to the Last Supper."*

Much of the Jerusalem area has been silted over so that there are places that Jesus walked that are now below the surface buried in up to 6 feet of silt. We had been told about the "Cum Sin" winds. This was a feature in the sky much like smog that we have due to automobile engine discharges. A darkening haze seen in the sky in Israel is not from automobile engine discharges, but rather it is the winds that they call, "Cum Sin". People wear a head cover not only to cover their head, but so it can to be adapted to also cover their nostrils when the Cum Sin wind is raging. It is the settling of this fine dust over centuries that has caused much of the area, where Jesus walked, to be covered with soil. Thus archaeologists have "digs" to discover lost civilizations.

We visited the Garden of Gethsemane just before we went to the place of the Last Supper. It's a small garden of perhaps an acre or two. The olive trees still growing there are thought to include some of the original trees which grew there in Jesus times. They were short trees with very large hollow trunks. Like all trees, olive tree growth is around the outside, but olive trees continue to grow even as the center has hollowed out and disappeared. The Kidron Valley separates this unique old garden from Old Jerusalem.

Jesus walked only the short distance down to the Kidron Valley to then walk up the limestone stair-steps leading to the place of the Last Supper. The stair-steps were in a location where the winds would keep the steep stairs from being covered with silt; therefore this was told to be the only place still unmolested where it is certain that we can truly say that Jesus walked.

Although the guide merely mentioned this fact about the steps as he was passing, I will always be perplexed as to why no one else wanted to walk on the very steps where Jesus walked. The group did wait for me at the bus because this was the day that I RAN UP THE STAIRS WHERE JESUS WALKED! "WOW."

Wow #2

We were taken to the north end of the Sea of Galilee. On this day it was a calm, blue lake. I stood there in awe. This is where Jesus calmed the water and walked on the water. In my mind the often seen painting of Jesus walking on the water and calming the storm appeared in my imagination.

Near the edge of the lake was erected a bronze statue of Jesus laying hands on Peter as Peter, kneeling on his knee, is bowed before Jesus. It was the great commission statue. This is the place where Jesus told Peter, "Feed my sheep".

We were told that this also was the place where Jesus fed the five thousand. It is deduced that since there are seven springs flowing nearby, this must have been the place. It is logical that if five thousand people ate bread and fish, they would need to be in a place with adequate drinking water.

Near the statue was a meditation circle or campfire circle, but without a burning fire on this day. Our group sat on the stone seats of the circle almost under the statue of Jesus and Peter. Our group sang songs that we all had known since childhood. I was so choked up with awe that I could not sing. I could only think, "WOW."

Wow #3

We had just finished walking the Via Dela Rosa (the way of Christ), which is thought to be the path Jesus took carrying the cross before his crucifixion. Our guide walked up to a door of a brown brick building and a Catholic nun appeared. Our guide paid her and we entered a Jesuit convent. We walked down into a lower level, which we were told had been excavated after the convent was built. Four to six feet of soil had been removed to expose the "pavement" mentioned in John 19:13. There is only one place in the Bible that mentions the word, "pavement". I suspect that in the time of Christ, there were very few places in Jerusalem that were paved. This pavement had been outside of Pilot's headquarters. The pavement is made of smooth limestone tablets making a pavement just as smooth as the concrete pavements we have now.

This is the location where Pilot brought Jesus out after questioning him in his headquarters and told the crowd that he found no fault in Him. It is here where the crowds shouted, "Crucify Him". It is here that the Roman soldiers cast their lot for Jesus' clothes and put a crown of thorns on His head.

Previous to this time, Pilot had caused the Jews to riot because he had taken tax money intended for the Jewish temple and with that money, Pilot built an aqueduct. As a result Rome was not happy with Pilot at this time. Pilot knew that if he could not keep the Jews calm to prevent another uprising, he could be removed from his place of authority by the Romans. As a result, he did not want to go against the crowds, even though he was sentencing an innocent man to death.

Pilot had several hundred Roman soldiers under his command to be used to police the Jewish people. This was a time of slavery and many of these soldiers owned Jewish slaves to do their bidding. It is thought that during those times that the soldiers did not have specific orders from Pilot, but were still on duty, they would gather there on the pavement in front of Pilot's quarters awaiting orders from him.

When we walked down the stairs below the convent, there was a cistern to the left of the stairs to catch rainwater. Small waterways in the shape of our eaves-troughs were cut in the limestone pavement to lead the water to the cistern. Almost in the very center of the paved floor was located a roped-off place that prevented anyone from stepping on the small "fox and goose" type of carving in the pavement.

"Fox and goose" was a game we played outside in the new-fallen snow when I was a child at country school. We made a circle by tromping a round trail in the snow. Then we dissected the circle with trails making four equal quarters out of the circle. The center intersection was the "free" area and a student could not be "caught" by the person who had been tagged "it". This was a limited game of tag.

The circle carved on the pavement was about three feet in diameter and it had the same shape as our "fox and goose" circle in the snow at country school. We were told that this was where the Roman soldiers played the "King's Game". It is unknown to me exactly how the game is played but whoever lost the game became "King" for the day. A mock crown was placed on his head and a kingly robe was placed on his shoulders. He was then paraded through the streets of Jerusalem while being mocked as a King. At the end of the day he was executed. The game was like a game of "Russian roulette". It was a gruesome and hideous game.

We were told that just prior to the time of Christ's crucifixion, Pilot made a rule that his soldiers could no longer play the game of King for a Day. The reason was that he was losing too many good soldiers. However, the soldiers found a way around Pilot's rules. They continued playing the game with less somber consequences to them personally. If a soldier lost in the game now, he did not lose his life at the end of the day, rather his slave was executed in his stead.

I stood and looked at that circle in the pavement as this story was told. I wondered how many Romans lost their lives because of this circle carved on the limestone pavement. I wondered how many Jewish slaves lost their lives because of this circle. And finally I wondered what part, if anything, this circle had to do with the way Christ was treated and eventually crucified. I thought, "WOW."

Wow #4

We entered a chapel in Bethlehem that was shaped like a rotunda. Not a large chapel, it was perhaps thirty feet in diameter. They told us that this is located in the place where Jesus was born. We stood in a circle and held hands while we sang Christmas carols though the month was March, not December. Unlike my previous experience on the Sea of Galilee, I was not emotionally affected in this place. Though this was a chapel, somehow it did not seem to have that certain feeling of authenticity, even as it was claimed to be the place of Christ's birth. This time I was able to sing Christmas carols with the group as we held hands in a circle.

When we left the chapel, the bus was not readily available, so some of our group explored the area. We proceeded several hundred feet behind the chapel to find a cave. A little black-bearded man in clerical clothes was standing in front of the mouth of the cave. He beckoned us, *"Come in, come in, come into my cave and I will tell you the story of the cave."*

The mouth or opening of the cave was concave, about 8 feet high at the center of the opening. The opening of the cave was about 30 or 40 feet wide with the roof of the cave extending down from the center apex of the opening to the ground at each end. The cave extended perhaps 40 feet back into the hill with the roof receding from the height of about 8 feet at its apex, down to the ground floor at the rear of the cave . The interior of the cave was shaped like half of a dome cut into the hill.

Our group crowded into the little cave. The little priest stood on one side of the cave behind a white linen-covered altar with a cross in the center. The little priest spoke: *"I am a French Jesuit priest. I welcome you into this little cave. There are other caves in the vicinity similar to this cave. It is not actually known exactly in which cave the Christ Child was born. As you look out in the grassy valley below this cave, you can see where the shepherds were when the angels came. These shepherds were not ordinary shepherds; they were special shepherds since the offspring of the ewes from their flocks were used as sacrificial lambs at the temple. These were special flocks and special shepherds. Whenever there was inclement weather or when marauding animals might endanger their flock, the shepherd would herd his sheep and goats into these caves for protection. He would build an open fire near the front of the cave at night to ward off the animals and to warm the cave."*

I stood near the center of the cave since the roof of the cave receded and I liked to stand where my head did not touch the ceiling.

The priest went on: *"If you look up to the ceiling of the cave, you will see that the ceiling is covered with black soot. That soot is the accumulation of more than 2000 years of bonfires built in this cave by shepherds who tend their flocks for sacrificial lambs."*

I reached up to touch the ceiling. A piece of black soot about an inch square fell into the palm of my hand. I felt I had molested this sacred place and if I could have, I would have replaced that piece of history back on the ceiling. At this time I had a feeling that this must be the place of the birth of Christ.

The little man with a black beard went on: *"Would you like to hear me sing Silent Night?"* Of course, we all clapped. With a deep baritone voice he sang the song first in English and then in French. We were all moved. This was a very special place. This Jesuit Priest was a very special person.

As we left, the little priest stepped outside and as each of us passed by him on our way leaving the cave, he grasped our right hand in both of his. Then he looked up into our eyes with the loving eyes of one who knows Christ and said to each of us with a smile, "May God Bless You".

I had just received a rare experience. I realized that this little Jesuit priest was part of God's magnificent plan. Was it not His plan that we should pass the story of the Christ child from one person to another person until everyone knows that saving story?

God's plan is that the greatest story ever told should continue to be told and handed on from one loving Christian to another evermore until the end of time.

"WOW."

Chapter Eleven

Parental Admonitions

The story of President George Washington, who chopped down the cherry tree, is an example for everyone to always tell the truth. My school-teacher mother was a devoted adherent of the premise of the George Washington Cherry Tree Story. She told me many, many times that I must always tell the truth.

One time when I was of preschool age, my mother and I had gone to the Brush Creek Store, which was a handy one-room neighborhood place to buy the basic groceries or some miscellaneous mercantile items. I ignored the adults in the room and proceeded to examine the small hardware items openly displayed on the counter. I picked up one small item and was curious as to its purpose, since I had never before seen anything similar. I had the item in my hand when my mother suddenly ushered me out of the store to return home. She had purchased a few groceries while I was attempting to learn what task this little item had been designed to accomplish. To this day I still have no idea what this little item was intended to do.

When we got home and my mother discovered that I had shoplifted this little item, I soon learned in no uncertain terms that one must never take anything from a store without paying for it. We immediately drove back to Brush Creek (often called Podunk by the locals) to return the item. My mother profusely expressed her apology and I was made to do the same in no uncertain terms. It must have been a really good lesson taught. I yet remember it 84 years later.

My parents, Joseph and Elsie Johnson.

Just recently I received an e-mail from my good friend, David Hanson, who now is the managing officer of an American manufacturing plant in China. Dave had been an engineer for his company in Owatonna, Minnesota. He started his e-mail by saying that honesty is a good attribute to practice, but he had discovered why it really is an absolute necessity, as he went on to tell the story. David explained that he had an unstated, continuing opinion of the president of the company as being a "nasty" corporate president. He had harshly piled on staff members to get better "numbers" than they had projected in their outlook statements. In response to his prodding attempts, David in the past had actually always told him what he understood to be the *truth* often at a painful whack to his ego. He had always felt that the president enjoyed abusing him, until one day in early 2003.

David was personally asked to sit in on a meeting with all the division presidents. They were asked for their opinions, as to whether the company should build an overseas plant in China and they were to give their reasons for or against this possibility.

David happened to sit on the president's right side. Each person spoke in turn clockwise until they came to him. David was not a division president, but only an engineer. After all the division presidents had spoken, the president said, *"David, you are probably wondering why you are here with this group. You are here because you are the only one at this table who has never lied to me. I respect your opinion."* Pretty high praise for trying to keep the boss on the right path!

David's opinion was blunt, *"It is my opinion that we are about five years late in going to China."* David knew that their competitors were already operating in China, but he suspected that his answer was not the one the president wanted to hear. All the others around the table actually knew that David was right, but each of them had a habit of lying to the president, just to get him off the phone for the moment. This time they would pay a big price for giving the opinion that they suspected the president wanted to hear.

Shortly after that meeting, the president asked David to build the new plant in China. He was directed to purchase the equipment needed, hire the people to operate the equipment, and then manage the operation.

David's dedication to my mother's admonition of "always tell the truth" is the basis of his success, not only as an administrative manager, but also as a person who has earned the respect of all who know him.

My father had a slightly different take on this subject and approached my mother's admonition from a different angle based on his own negative experience, learned the hard way and never forgotten. He had recently returned from serving in the Navy during the First World War in 1918. He was newly married and was starting farming with meager funds for the venture. All farmers at that time had horses, raised a few hogs and chickens, and milked a few cows. The neighborhood creamery was only a half-mile away from his farm and the cream check was expected to be a primary source of his income.

Saturday night was the customary night for farmers and their wives to do the weekly shopping in town. The stores stayed open until nine or ten for the conveniencc of the farm families to shop after completing their evening chores. It was a community social event, a chance to talk to acquaintances in stores and on the sidewalk of the main street. Once each week, they would need necessary staples that were not produced on the farm or in the garden.

On this Saturday evening my father desperately needed a milk strainer to strain the milk that he poured into the top of the DeLaval cream separator. The strainer cost was three dollars at the hardware store. Dad asked the owner of the store, if he could charge the three dollars until next week when he would get his first cream check from the creamery.

My father's older brother, Orin, was one whose conscience was not always successful in guiding him to make good decisions. The stories my father told about his brother were plentiful and always ended in Orin making the wrong choice.

During the Great Depression, Orin married a lovely woman and fathered seven children. After dark one night, Orin sold the

50 chickens that his wife had been feeding all summer for food for their family. He and the chickens were gone the next day and he was never seen by his family again. This painful story was an example of the many poor choices Orin had made.

On that Saturday night my father asked for credit for one week to buy the milk strainer at the hardware store. The owner replied with a question, *"What's your name?"* When my father answered, the owner bluntly replied, *"We don't give credit to Johnsons".* My father instantly knew that it was his brother who had given the family a bad name, one that labeled the name Johnson, to be a person who was untrustworthy.

Often in my youth my father advised me, *"Victor, your name is the most valuable thing you have. You can't buy it; you have to earn it."*

Much later I wrote a recommendation for Art Koskovich to be inducted into the Minnesota Aviation Hall of Fame. Art had taught himself to fly and, although he limped with one leg and had one arm that was practically useless because of having polio as a child, yet he became an avid pilot and aviation enthusiast. For five dollars each, on a Sunday afternoon, Art Koskovich gave Duffy Erdahl and me our first airplane rides in a small two-place Ercoupe. That was the day that each of us decided that one day we would fly our own airplanes, if ever we could afford it.

Before World War II, Art had been the moving force to start the Blue Earth Airport, which is located between Elmore and Blue Earth, Minnesota. Before and during the war he was the full-time manager of the airport. As an instructor in the Civil Air Patrol, he spoke at many high schools in the area encouraging students to become engaged in aviation and become members of the CAP. Art Koskovich had "earned his good name".

Although Art had been told that his nomination was going to be accepted, unfortunately Art died several months before the actual induction event. The night of the induction, I made the nomination posthumously and many of his family were there to hear the announcement of the honor at the Thunderbird Hotel in Minneapolis. One of those who had traveled almost 200 miles to be there was a former secretary at my law office. She was the widow of one of Art's deceased sons. I had not seen her for at least 10 or maybe 15 years.

After the ceremony, we hugged and spoke about times past. Nancy paid me the extreme compliment that night. She said that working for me had been the most enjoyable job she had ever experienced in her lifetime. She had heard that I had lost my wife to Alzheimer's disease and she expressed her sympathy. It was good to see her again and I was thrilled with the compliment.

Nancy now lived in Algona, Iowa and had remarried after her husband, John, had died. She had experienced living alone and by the time I met her again that night at the Thunderboard Hotel, she was experiencing the joy and love of a new life partner.

At a later time, I had coffee with Nancy at the coffee shop in Algona. She offered the name, Eleanor Lindeman, and told me I should call her some day for some "companionship". During her teaching career, Eleanor had taught some of Nancy's children and lived only a couple blocks from Nancy.

I wasn't ready for anything like that. I thought that when one is over the age of 70, one does not telephone a previously unknown lady for a date. It seemed to me that at my age, not only would that be difficult, it would be impossible. I had already decided that now that I was single, I was going to do what I wanted to do, when I wanted to do it, and if I did it, I was not going to compromise with anyone.

I tried to forget the idea of Eleanor Lindeman. But I didn't really forget that idea. Two weeks later after eating my cold noon meal alone, I thought about Nancy's suggestion. Might be fun, I thought. What the heck, she lives an hour south in Algona, Iowa and I don't know her. She can only tell me to hit the road and since I will never meet her on the street or meet her socially, I'll not ever suffer any embarrassment. If I try calling her for a coffee date and it doesn't happen, I can forget about Eleanor Lindeman, and that's OK since I have never seen her and I wouldn't even know her if I passed her on the street.

In the call, I offered to meet her at the coffee shop in Algona for a cup of coffee that afternoon. She declined, said she couldn't do that. I wondered why. Much later I found out that it was at this coffee shop that she and her best friend, Linda, enjoyed breakfast together every morning before Linda taught school. The owner of the place was Gwen, who also was a very close friend to Linda and Eleanor.

The real reason she would not meet me at that coffee shop was that she had never even seen me before. Maybe I could be a little short, bald guy with bib-overalls and long whiskers using a corn-cob pipe. Maybe I would come in an old rusted-out pickup truck. She could not take the chance because she knew Gwen would serve her and ask questions. Maybe other of her friends might happen to come for coffee at the same time and see her with this strange man. So she said, *"Why don't you just come to my house for coffee?"*

I answered, *"I never expected that invitation when I called, but I'll be there in an hour."*

Just to be on the safe side, Eleanor locked all the doors and was in an upstairs window looking out when I drove up. She looked and thought, *"Well, the car is pretty nice. He seems tall and well dressed."* She made the determination to unlock the front door and invite me in. We sat on the sofa in the living room with coffee for two hours, each of us trying to find out just who this new person was and what he or she was all about. Yet we were trying not to be too direct to be offensive with the questions we had developed in our minds.

It was after 5 and going on 6 PM, when I invited her to accompany me to a restaurant of her choosing. After this much time together, Eleanor had decided it was acceptable to be seen with me in a public place. The afternoon had passed rapidly and the conversation had gone wonderfully well. I realized that a fortunate guy over age 70, like me, still can successfully date a woman he had never met. But at the time, because of our inexperience, we both were asking ourselves, "What do we do next?" We were like the dog that chased a car and, when it stopped, didn't know what to do.

At the end of that first day of introducing ourselves to each other, that real question of what to do next was delicately touched upon, since we were both a bit emotionally over-charged. As we parted that evening, we mutually agreed that our next contact obligation would be by e-mail. Somehow we might determine the answer to our unanswered question, "What do we do next?"

On Thursday, the next morning, Eleanor met Linda for early breakfast at the coffee shop before Linda went to school. Guess what the conversation was about that morning. Linda asked, *"How could you? You didn't know anything about this guy. It could have been dangerous."* So Linda was told about locking the doors and observing him before deciding to open. Besides, Eleanor said that she had found out during the initial phone conversation that he knew of Deb Manske, who was a teacher with Linda in Algona. He obviously knew Nancy Hugo, who had been his legal secretary. Both came from Blue Earth and it's a smaller town than Algona. He couldn't have been known as being too bad.

I think it may have been an exciting conversation that day in the coffee shop, but what do I know? I wasn't there, but I can imagine it quite well, having often watched and listened as they discuss everything and everybody when we have met Linda for lunch or coffee in Algona.

After hearing about Vic Johnson for the first time, Linda offered, *"Today when I'm at school, I'll ask Deb Manske about this guy and see what she thinks of him."*

Eleanor responded, *"You be sure to call me right after school this afternoon before you go home and let me know what she says. Now you tell me the truth. Let me know what kind of a person he is even if it's bad."*

Eleanor went home. Linda went to school. It wasn't ten minutes before Eleanor's phone rang. It was Linda. There was no way she could wait until after school to report this news to Eleanor. *"Well, what did she say?"* anxiously asked Ellie. "

Deb said to hang on to him. *"He's a keeper. He's a close friend of my father and he took very good care of his wife who died of Alzhiemer's disease."*

Obviously this was not the end of the story, but only the beginning of a much longer story. Eleanor broke the ice on Thursday afternoon, the next day after we first met, with an invitation by e-mail for me to come to her home on Friday, the following evening for a home-cooked meal.

Things progressed quite rapidly after that meal as we often found things to do together, and conversation no longer needed to be as guarded as on that initial day when the "unknowns" first found each other.

After two weeks of whirlwind days of finding places to go and things to do, I broke all protocol, when I surprised her by offering my hand in marriage on bended knee with an engagement ring.

Eleanor was flabbergasted and unprepared, when she immediately accepted. Our excuse for the speedy timeline was "our age" which excuse was similar to and just as facetious as the tongue-in-cheek excuse not to buy green bananas.

Victor Johnson and Eleanor Lindeman.

On the day that Eleanor's friend, Linda, questioned her at school concerning the name, Vic Johnson, I had not yet personally met Deb Manske, the person who assuredly knew the name and sealed my future. I only knew her father well because he had been a friend since childhood, and also had been a life-long resident of Blue Earth.

So my story proves my father's admonition to be absolutely true. Over the many years of my life, I had earned something of great value. It was beyond my wildest imaginations that acceptance of my parents' admonitions would pay such huge dividends. Linda and Deb only uncovered the simple truth that I owned a VALUABLE NAME that I had protected during my entire lifetime and all the community knew.

Chapter Twelve

Community

My great-grandfather, Ole Iverson, in 1861 came west on a dirt road called Highway number 9 (Faribault County Highway 16). He had a new bride, a wagon, a team of horses and a plow as he came to choose a parcel of land 6 miles east of Blue Earth as his new home. Because of the new Homestead Act he could receive some of the previously unplowed prairie grassland free if he would live on it and improve the land for 5 years. For his first home that summer he dug a hole in the ground. Around that hole, he laid bricks made from the root-tangled sod that was all around on this vast prairie. He attached a makeshift roof over their new sod house. There they lived through the first winter until later when they could complete a log house. Ole and his bride, Brita, eventually had 11 children, 6 of whom lived to adulthood. To be pioneers in this new area where the prairie soil had never before been cultivated was a difficult and hazardous life for Ole and Brita (who later became known as Britha) and their children who survived.

Twenty-seven years later, my grandfather, Ole Johnson, had just immigrated from his home in Norway. He walked west down that same dirt road called Highway number 9 having gotten off the train at Wells, Minnesota. He knew no one here in America in this area. In his hand he had a satchel with his belongings and in his pocket he had seventy-five cents remaining from the expense of the long trip from Norway. He was tired and hungry when he came to the big white house that Ole and Britha Iverson had built to replace the log house and the sod house that they had lived in 27 years before. That white house was built very close to Highway number 9. The red barn that Ole Iverson had built was close on the opposite side of the road. This had been a customary way of locating buildings back in Norway so that all the farm buildings would be convenient to the road between.

Britha was a hard-working pioneer housewife that baked loaves of bread twice a week for her husband and their growing family of six now nearing adulthood. It was her habit to set the loaves out on the south window sill to cool. It is a family story that has been passed down, that when Ole and Britha first moved into the big new white house, Indians that were passing by on the dirt road number 9 would see and smell the wonderful aroma of the fresh baked loaves of bread. They would then trade seeds for a loaf of bread with Britha. Because of her bread, she was friends with the Indians before the historic Indian uprising, which is part of the history of this area.

Twenty-seven years after the Iversons' arrival in Faribault County, Ole Johnson walked from the train depot at Wells, MN on Highway 9 until he came to the white Iverson farm home where he saw and smelled the same wonderful aroma of the fresh baked bread that the Indians had smelled. When he inquired about the bread, being a Norwegian like the Iversons, he was invited in for lunch.

It also is a family story that has been passed down through the years, that on that first day at the Iverson home he was so hungry that he ate a WHOLE loaf of bread with homemade plum jam. He must have noticed the next to the youngest daughter, Martha Iverson, in that room that first day. Martha became my grandmother. Grandfather Ole Johnson and his bride, Martha, soon built a new home with a complete set of farm buildings next door to and located as part of the original Iverson homestead acreage.

It was there that Ole and Martha Johnson farmed and raised their family of five children; thus it was where my father lived as a child. It much later became the place where I have since lived and raised our family after I moved back to Blue Earth in 1954.

My parents, Joseph and Elsie Johnson, purchased the original Iverson white home and farm buildings from the Iverson heirs after his grandparents died. It was there they lived as long as they were able and it was there that I lived and grew as a child.

It was when I was about 14 or 15 years of age that I first learned the importance as well as the obligations of belonging to a neighborhood community.

This was at a time that every farmer had 5 or more acres of alfalfa to be harvested 3 times in the summer. It was a job that always required more than one person to move the crop from the field into the big haymow above the cows and horses. My father and our next door neighbor, Alvin Erickson, always helped each other to harvest and store it in each barn. One would drive the horses and wagon straddling the windrow in the field. The hay loader on the rear of the wagon would elevate it into the wagon as the other man on the load with a 3-tined fork would level it to make a nicely stacked load on the hay rack.

After the load was driven beside the big barn, one of the men had to be in the haymow to receive the hay as it arrived. The man on the ground would attach the ropes located under the hay on the wagon to the hay carrier mechanism, which was attached to a long heavy rope to lift the hay up to just under the roof of the barn.

A third person (usually the housewife, but as I grew taller I got the job) would drive the team of horses to pull the big long barn rope that reached inside of the barn and all the way along the top of the barn and back down to the loaded hayrack. As the horses pulled that big rope forward away from the barn, the large "sling" of hay would rise vertically up from the wagon to the big barn door near the roof. When it reached the roof above the wagon, the hay carrier would roll rapidly on the steel tracks hanging just under the roof which extended the length of the barn. When the carrier reached the desired spot in that big haymow, the man in the haymow would shout, "NOW" to tell the man outside who would jerk the trip rope causing the hay to fall to the intended spot. It then had to be moved with a 3-tined fork to the sides of the haymow to eventually fill the barn almost to the very top of the building with the sweet smelling alfalfa hay. To me it was a wonderful operation that still entertains my memories.

I have a memory of one of those long summer days when daylight lasts far into the evening and our work for the day was done when I returned to that sweet-smelling alfalfa hay stacked almost to the very top of the barn with barely enough headroom to walk. Sitting high atop the hay, and using my imagination, I gazed out through the big open barn door to survey the lush green fields and peer as far as I could to see beyond the wooded river bottom land which was a quarter mile away. I squinted my eye through the imaginary eyepiece of a large long telescope. My imagination allowed me to survey the countryside perhaps all the way to Iowa. Today, to recall that moment, I need my imagination once again to remember the sweet smell of the fresh alfalfa hay and to recall the distant scene I saw in my youth from my high perch atop the completely filled haymow.

As a young lad, I drove our team of buckskin horses, Maude and Toots, to mow our field of alfalfa hay with our five-foot sickle mower. Maude was a 'line follower' and would walk along the edge of the uncut alfalfa hay so that I did not need to steer the horses except around the corners as I mowed around and around the field until I finished in the center. I sat on the red iron seat of the Mc-Cormick Deering mower. That seat did not remain still, but rather would vibrate violently as the sickle of the machine rapidly went back and forth. Sitting at the table for the evening meal, the bottom of my anatomy would be numb from the vibration. By the end of the meal I would heal as the numbness left and my feeling back there would return.

Maude died, as did one of Alvin's horses that he needed when he mowed his hay. So for one summer, both Alvin and I mowed hay with our Toots and with Lady, the remaining horse that Alvin owned. Without Maude, it took more effort to mow hay, because I now had to be alert and steer the horses all of the time. The "one horse per neighbor" situation lasted only one summer. My father bought a tractor mower with a seven-foot sickle to be mounted solid to the wide rear drawbar of our F-20 Farmall tractor. The mower had a free-turning castor rubber tire at the rear. This arrangement located the mower sickle about three feet behind the rear tractor wheel. Because of this, I soon learned that I needed to drive extremely straight because if I would turn the front of the tractor to the left, the solid-mounted sickle bar located three feet behind the tractor would pivot accordingly to the right. This made a new challenge for me to master.

I no longer sat on a vibrating seat behind the horses when I mowed our hay. To me it was fun to mow hay with the tractor and I became quite adept at mowing hay with the new rig.

I made two goals for myself as I worked with the big new 7-foot mower.

Goal #1 As I mowed the field I would not leave a single strand of alfalfa unmowed in the entire field, requiring me to drive perfectly straight along the side of the standing hay. I would not let the sickle bar plug up with a bunch of cut hay because a few plants of alfalfa would then be left unmowed.

Goal #2 I would mow the entire field without touching the throttle to slow down or stop.

This was fun for a young teenage 'hotshot' that liked to drive fast. It meant that when I turn at the corner of the square field, I must begin the turn about 5 or 6 feet before the sickle bar reaches the corner. At that exact location and moment, I must turn the knob on the steering wheel very rapidly to the right as the sickle bar behind the tractor would swing around to the left 90 degrees to catch the remaining 5 or 6 foot strip of uncut hay. Then I must rapidly turn left to precisely follow the edge of the standing hay again. My challenge was to do this without slowing at the corner, without plugging the sickle with mowed hay, and without leaving a single plant of alfalfa unmowed. For me it was a neat challenge and I became quite adept at my little game. My father had watched and realized that I enjoyed doing the job without making mistakes, so after that he always delegated me to do the hay mowing.

One day my father ordered me as follows: "*Victor,* (he never called me Vic) *Alvin Erickson wants to mow his hay today. I want you to take the F-20 and the mower to his place and mow his alfalfa hay for him. You drive right through his yard. Don't even stop. Mow the field south of his buildings. When you get finished and return back through his farm yard, Alvin will stop you and want to pay you. You do NOT accept any money from Alvin.*"

I answered, "*OK, Dad.*"

I did a perfect job of mowing that field that day. I never touched the throttle to slow down and there was not a singe spear of alfalfa left uncut because of a "plug-up." When I finished to return through the Erickson yard, it happened just as my Dad had said. Alvin came out, leaned on the big tire of the F-20 and offered me a 5-dollar bill.

At this time of my capitalistic life, my entire net worth was $35 and one Hiawatha bicycle. Five dollars would have been a substantial improvement to my savings account and my feeling of well being. I was not even tempted. I said, *"No, Alvin, you can't pay me. I did this for you because I wanted to."* As I drove toward home, I felt really satisfied that I had refused the payment according to my father's instruction; then I thought about the reason I had given for refusing the payment which added to my satisfaction. I smiled as I returned home while thinking about it. I have often relived the satisfaction of that incident since that day. It was that day early in my youth that I discovered the meaning of the word, community. To me it meant, "I did this for you because I wanted to."

When our house fire occurred in 1996, all our neighbors and friends in the community came the next day to help. We needed to empty the house of all of our accumulated belongings and put them in the barn and other outbuildings on the farm to be stored until we could decide what to do next. The house had to be empty to be rebuilt. Most of the belongings were smoke-damaged to some extent, but much could be salvaged later. The neighbors came to lug, carry and store all of our belongings accumulated over these many years. These were friends from our neighborhood community who had come to help us *"because they wanted to"*. One neighbor, Neil Tagatz, came from several miles away with his tractor and front-end loader that early morning. As I thought back, I had never spoken to this neighbor at length before. I had only responded to him as we passed each other, *"Hi, Neil".* Now he was here early the day after the fire to volunteer his help. It was his tractor that pulled our two burnt cars out of what was once an attached garage. The cars now were melted down from the heat to be only about 3 feet tall. We still had our little red S-10 Chevy pick-up for our only remaining transportation. It had been stored safely in the barn at the time of the fire.

Our home before the fire.

Our home after the fire, July 9,1996.

Six of my son's friends from Minneapolis drove down with my son, Matthew, to help us on a Saturday after the fire. Three of us went up on the roof of the house with chain saws to cut the damaged roof into 6-foot square slabs and drop them into a big dump truck to be burned. We previously had hired a big backhoe to dig a large burning pit in the old "cattle yard" behind the barn. The other helpers from Minneapolis removed wet soggy carpeting and crumbled particleboard from the floors to be loaded into the dump truck to be burned. One man brought a drawing board and sitting on the back of a pickup truck with my directions redrew the floor plan of the second floor because I had envisioned some changes I might make when I rebuilt our damaged bedrooms on the second floor.

One neighbor, Barney Bauman, came for 3 days and removed the damaged siding from the house. Although he limped with a game leg, he was more than willing to climb the scaffolding to remove the siding from the house.

When we began to rebuild, two neighbors, Glen and Jim Skogen, came and helped shingle the new roof that carpenters had rebuilt. Two more neighbors, Gary Meyer and Bobbie Werner, helped me put new siding on the house.

Later on a day when I was finishing the garage by applying the roof shingles, my friend, Gary Meyer, came uninvited and said, *"I thought you needed help."* He stayed and helped that day until together we finished the garage roof.

Friends and neighbors from our community organized a benefit pancake luncheon to raise funds for our belongings lost in the fire. Can you in your wildest imagination think that a community might have a benefit luncheon to raise funds for an ATTORNEY? They must have forgotten about all those bad lawyer jokes. They came, they ate, they donated and we celebrated each other's presence. That's the wonderful nature of our community.

I knew I would need to make a lot of trips to the lumberyards for material to rebuild our house that according to the insurance company was "totaled." I had just purchased a 16-foot tandem trailer to pull behind my little red S-10 Chevy pickup to haul those supplies from the lumberyard. I was going east that day on 6th Street in Blue Earth heading toward the lumberyard. I had just passed the old high school building and Salem Methodist Church when at the next corner, Bertha Kohlmeyer Ladien with her beautiful pristine white Lincoln town car went through the stop sign. The right front of the Lincoln collided with the left front of my little red S-10 Chevy pick-up. The ladies who were having Bible study at the Methodist parsonage across the street all came out to see what had caused the loud crash. They stood on the front porch and watched as Bertha and I got out of our cars. The juices were running out on the pavement from the radiators of the two vehicles. I walked around both automobiles to Bertha's side as she got out of her car. Bertha spoke, *"Oh Vic, I'm so sorry."*

I responded, *"Oh Bertha, I'm so sorry, too."* Then we both stood right there in the middle of the intersection and unabashedly hugged each other even as the Methodist ladies on the porch watched.

When the policeman had made his report and called for the tow truck, Bernie Kriewall came. Bernie, like everyone else in our community, knew about our devastating fire. His words as he shook his head in disbelief were, *"Well Vic, your luck has got to turn better pretty soon."*

One day during this time I walked down the main street of Blue Earth past one of the gift shops. The owner, Valerie Blumenshein, is of a younger generation and was a member of a different church than ours and we had never had occasion to previously meet socially except in her store, so we knew only of her pleasant personality and smile. Our devastating fire had been the talk of the community, so as I walked past her gift store that day, lovely Valerie came out, walked up to me and GAVE ME A HUG! I stood there on the sidewalk in front of her store totally surprised with my arms hanging limp at my side as she gave me that hug. I looked up to the clear sky to see where the moisture was coming from that showed up on my cheeks below my eyes as she hugged me and she said, *"Oh, Vic, I'm so sorry for the loss of your home."* That's an unexpected and unearned hug that occurred right there on the side walk of the main street of Blue Earth in front of her gift shop that I will long remember. I believe Valerie gave that hug *"because she wanted to."*

After suffering from Alzheimer's disease, Rene died on June 6, 2004. About five years before her death she had chosen to hang over our fireplace mantle as the centerpiece of the room, a beautiful ornately framed picture of Christ with the lost lamb on His shoulder. The hospital bed in which she died was temporarily located in front of that fireplace. One week later on Sunday June 13, she in her coffin was also located beneath the beautiful picture of Christ above the mantel when all the neighbors and friends respectfully came.

Rene in her lifetime had always been the consummate hostess. She loved the home I had built and then rebuilt for her after the fire. It was fitting to have the visitation or wake in the home she loved rather than having it in the funeral chapel on 14th Street in Blue Earth. She could "host" our community one last time. Approximately 400 people came to our home that sunny Sunday afternoon. They all took their turn to stand and reflect for a moment before her coffin *"because they wanted to."*

Debbie Ankeny and her two sisters-in-law, Patty Hague and Shelly Griemann sang as the special music that day that we celebrated Rene's life at the church. These ladies were the daughters and daughter-in-law of Scott Ankeny, who had been a high school classmate with Rene and me when we once were students in Blue Earth high school. Patty had been a kindergarten student back when Rene was her teacher. These ladies were formally dressed and as they stood before the congregation, they looked more beautiful than the pictures of movie stars I see in magazines. They sang the beloved song, "Amazing Grace," unaccompanied by any instruments. The first part was sung in unison and then they sang the last part in harmony. Angels could not have sung it more beautifully. Our family had kept our composure during the funeral service quite well until they sang that day and then our tears freely flowed.

I sent a card of thanks to each of the three ladies thanking them for their wonderful contribution of song at the celebration of Rene's life. I enclosed a monetary check in each of the cards as evidence of our appreciation. Several days later, I received a sympathy card in the mail from Debbie Ankeny. Debbie is a professional singer, who for years has accompanied the internationally famous Anne Murray, as her backup singer. Debbie wrote these words on the inside cover of that card: *"It was our pleasure to sing for you, we didn't do it for money, but thank you for thinking we were worth it."* She enclosed and returned the three checks I had previously sent to the three who sang so beautifully that day. When I opened the letter, read the words and saw the returned checks, I wept again.

When I read the lovely card and recognized the loving graciousness of the ladies that sang at the funeral, I recalled a day 60 years before, when I first learned the real meaning of the word, community, as I told Alvin Erickson after I mowed his hay, *"No Alvin, you can't pay me. I did it because I wanted to."*

I remember that Great-Grandfather Ole and Great-Grandmother Britha Iverson, who with all their hardships began living in a sod house were the first of our family to chose this community.

I remember my Grandfather, Ole Johnson, who walked down dirt highway 9, saw and smelled the fresh baked bread and married the Iverson daughter he saw that day for the first time. He too made a choice to come and make this community his own. My father, Joseph, and I did not choose this community. Like the corn, we just grew here where we were planted. Had I been given a choice, perhaps I would have made the mistake of choosing a place with a beautiful view of the mountains like Colorado or Montana; I would have made a really huge mistake since we would not have experienced the rich generosity of this wonderful community that gave, worked, and loved, because they wanted to!

Chapter Thirteen

Forced Landing

I double-checked the date in my old log book. It was a beautiful Sunday afternoon on August 22, 1982. It was the day that I successfully landed my Cessna Cardinal RG on a narrow Iowa country road while unable to see out of the windshield that had been totally covered with oil.

My wife and I had invited another couple, Gene and Sherl Ostermann, to accompany us on a trip to Waukon, IA to visit friends for the day. Sherl was a bit reticent about flying in a small plane and asked several questions about the safety of the airplane. I could tell by her quizzical grin that she was a bit nervous but yet agreed, since I'm sure she did not want to disappoint the rest of us. One of the things I assured her of was that the plane engine had been recently overhauled so that everything was *mechanically in top shape.*

The days are long in August. However in spite of that, my wife chose to leave about 4:30 in the afternoon sunshine for the short trip home. The weather was perfect without a cloud in the sky and the winds were negligible. Almost an hour into our west-bound flight home, I looked back at the ladies who seemed to be relaxed with their eyes closed in the rear seat as we droned along. When I glanced at my "co-pilot," Gene, it seemed that he actually was asleep since his head was uncomfortably less than upright.

That was when I was alerted to a drop of oil appearing high in the middle of the outside of the windshield. As I began to consider that oil drop and before I could summon a conclusion, there was a second drop and then a third as the first two drops started a streak downward on the windshield. By the time I notified my passengers, the windshield was substantially covered with streaks of oil. (This all was happening before the time I had installed the wonderful GPS avionics that could always give much information to make flying safer and more comfortable including the actual present location at all times.) All I knew about our present position was that we were approaching the city of Northwood, IA from the east.

I asked my passengers to study the landscape out of the side windows to see if they could identify anything that might suggest the location of that city and its airport. I had no idea what could possibly cause this massive oil leak and my mind was racing trying to decide what to do next. I began to imagine a serious engine seize-up and propeller stop requiring a dead-stick landing that I had often read about in flying magazines.

By now the windshield was completely covered with oil and forward vision had been totally eliminated. I began turning my course 30 degrees from side to side trying to look westward from the side windows in the futile hope that the Northwood airport would somehow magically appear on the landscape. Silence prevailed from all my now fully awakened passengers. At my request, they too were stretching their eyes searching for the airport. I recognized that the airport was on the east side of the city so it would not be necessary to fly over the city to get to the airport, but I had no estimate of the distance to the airport at the time.

As I watched out of the right side window, I saw a newly blacktopped country road that extended north one mile from a grove of trees and a small white country church with a steeple. I double-checked the road before I made a decision. There were no utility wires that crossed the road and no road signs along the sides of the road; in fact there actually were no farmsteads on either side of the entire one mile stretch of road. I knew what I had to do without any further delay since the Northwood airport was not yet visible.

I announced to my passengers that I intended to land on the road that we had just passed on the right side of the airplane and that I would make a 270 degree turn to the left to line up for landing to the north on what looked like a recently paved one-mile country road. I was at about 500 feet as we flew over the church and the trees. Since forward visibility was lost, I began to alternately look out of each side window to estimate whether my flight path would be lined up over the center of the narrow road. Looking side to side, I began a slow descent. My biggest problem was that I could not actually see the road once I passed the church. I could only see the ditches on either side of the road and the corn fields beyond. The next moments passed quickly as I constantly estimated the distance to the cornfield on each side knowing the road was somewhere underneath.

I actually didn't have time to consider it at the time, but I would estimate that this road must have been only about 40 feet wide and as I recall, this road had but a two-foot shoulder on each side. (All paved airport runways are at least 75 feet wide.) Going into the ditch with the airplane would have been catastrophic since the ditch was narrow and about 3 feet deep with fairly steep sides. This was absolutely no time for any mistakes nor was there any available time to correct any that might occur.

Whenever I am landing, I usually constantly check the airspeed while descending, since I know that airspeed is crucial to a good landing. But at this time I had been too busy looking out the side windows from side to side to even think about the airspeed. By now we had descended to about 50 feet over the road when the stall warning horn began to squawk. My wife shouted, *"Have you got the gear down?"*

"Yes", I said and smiled as I knowingly gave the throttle a slight push to increase the airspeed and silence the squawking.

In my mind I congratulated myself for my good luck. Since I had no time to view the airspeed indicator, that squawking had told me that I needed a very slight increase of airspeed. My mind went on, *"If I can find the road, we will be exactly at the right speed for a perfect landing."*

In the very next instant I glanced out of the right side window. The cornfield just beyond the ditch looked a bit too close. I automatically began to move the controls to the left, but it was too late; the plane's wheels were now rolling on the road. It was the softest nicest landing possible. I had landed safely in the right hand lane of the narrow road. I was lucky. Although I had intended to land in the center of the road that I couldn't see, we were safely on the road. The engine was clicking happily away just like every other landing. I shut it off quickly not knowing how soon the lack of oil might produce some terrible noises.

We all got out. Sherl, the passenger who had been mistrusting the flight that morning said, *"Vic, I'll ride with you anytime!"*

Shortly after the landing, a pickup truck pulling a trailer carrying a race car and a rack of tires on the front of the trailer stopped because the wings of the plane were nearly the same width as the road. The guys were blunt and not very nice. They told us we didn't belong on the road and if we didn't get the "blank" out of their way, they would run us off the road. Nice guys, indeed. There was no offer to help as we turned the plane so the tail of the plane extended out over the ditch with the wings parallel to the roadway. I set the brakes. I was happy to have the racers disappear southbound.

After removing the cowling to inspect everything, I could see nothing obviously amiss. From the tool box I always carry in the luggage compartment, I used cotton cloths to partially clean the windshield of the oil. Another car came and perhaps stopped to observe the 'disaster'. We asked how far it was to Northwood. They said it was perhaps seven miles and since they were going there, they would be happy to give us a lift. I sent my 3 passengers with the driver and asked Gene to bring 8 quarts of aviation oil from the airport since I knew 8 quarts to be the total contents of the oil sump. Fortunately Gene knew a friend in Northwood that graciously loaned an automobile to him for a few days.

When Gene and the ladies returned, I poured 4 quarts of oil into the engine. The dipstick indicated it was now full. To me this meant that I still had at least 3 quarts remaining in the engine sump when I landed. I had been told that the engine can still keep circulating the oil with only 2 quarts remaining. The engine had been saved. But where did the leak originate?

With more rags that Gene had brought, we cleaned the windshield quite well. I now reasoned that because the airplane could not stay out on the road over night, and *since* I now had learned to land an airplane without forward vision just as 'Lucky' Lindberg had done in France, and *since* the grass runway at Northwood was much wider than the 40 foot roadway, and because the airplane was full of oil to capacity, I would take a calculated risk to fly the 6 or 7 miles to Northwood, but this time I would be alone in the airplane.

The landing at Northwood was uneventful. I only had received perhaps one or two drops of oil on the windshield. With that in mind, I had reasoned correctly, that wherever the oil leak was, the metal had contracted and closed partially after the engine had cooled off. My next decision would be whether to leave the airplane there or fly it 20 miles northward to my mechanic in Albert Lea. Perhaps this decision was quite questionable, one that perhaps a more cautious pilot would not make. I reasoned that if I only received one or two drops on the windshield in 7 miles of flight, surely I could fly 20 miles in about 10 minutes to my destination. I would not likely lose the 6 quarts of oil that would damage the engine. I would start with a completely cooled engine. All the country roads are a mile apart on the way to Albert Lea and I had now acquired an ability to land on a country road. The checkerboarded roads in the corn belt of the Midwest provide a possible landing strip in every mile.

N1843Q Cessna Cardinal RG.

The landing at Albert Lea was considered uneventful since I had a wide runway. I'll admit that the windshield was completely covered with oil again, yet the engine clicked happily away as I shut it down. With a bit of pent-up emotion I slammed the door shut, like the bad attitude of a jilted lover.

The problem was later discovered to be the steel oil line that connected the governor on the rear of the engine with the housing immediately behind the propeller. Like an automobile brake line, the oil line is made out of a flat piece of steel that was rolled into a small round pipe with a full-length welded seam. The mechanic that had overhauled the plane had neglected to replace one rubber-covered oil line support clamp. The engine design required two support clamps for the oil line. Because of that mechanic's omission, the constant vibration of the engine on the unsupported oil line caused a tiny split on the welded seam.

When I telephoned to confer with the mechanic in Wisconsin who had done the overhaul, I was told that he was unavailable since he recently had been killed in an accident when he flew freight over Georgia. He had not been quite high enough to clear the top of a mountain. Perhaps he had been neglectful once more, but I'll never know.

Chapter Fourteen

What Would Duffy Do?

Who but I can slice through God's billowed legs,
and laugh as I pass His cumulous castles?
Who else has seen His unclimbed peaks?
The rainbow's secret?
The real reason birds sing?
Because I fly, I envy no man on earth.
- Grover C. Norwood USAF (Retired)

We lived at a time when the Great Depression caused farm families to help each other as neighbors, which made those in the neighborhood dependent on each other. Farmers exchanged time, labor and tools freely. Farm wives prepared food for the threshers who came each August. They also worked along with their husbands and family in the labor of the farm enterprise.

Saturday night was a night for farmers to go to Blue Earth, MN to socialize on Main Street and buy supplies for the week. But Thursday night was the free show night and the time to socialize and purchase groceries at Frost, MN.

The Frost free show would begin as soon as it became dark on Thursday evenings. People brought blankets to sit on the lawn to watch the moving picture show in an empty lot across from Issacson's grocery store. Folding camp chairs either had not been invented or perhaps they were something that need not be purchased, since these were times that every penny in the purse was used conservatively. Besides, everyone could have a blanket to sit

Adorphus (Duffy) Erdahl.

upon. Every third week was a "cowboy movie". Such was the entertainment and social customs of the time during the Depression.

Duffy Erdahl (Adorphus Erdahl) and I began our lifetime relationship about the time I was 5 years old. Farm places at the time were at least a half mile apart and neither of us had siblings. I remember begging my Mom to let me go to play with Duffy. This happened most often in the summer time when we could play outside. However, I remember several times that we used the hill behind Duffy's house as a sliding hill. Every kid at that time had a sled for sliding. Since I did not have a hill at my home, I would run and flop down on the sled on a very slight slope in an attempt to get a short ride. I remember my sled finally became unusable because the support for the steel runners could not stand the continual hard "flop" as I was running as fast as I could, and the runners folded hopelessly under the wooden platform.

Duffy and I both started school at District 37, a one-room neighborhood country school, which eventually became the Emerald township hall. Often I have since gone to vote there, and I am impressed with the smallness of the room that held a large wood and coal fired stove and about 20 students from grades 1 through 8.

As a new first grade student, the most impressive part of the school to me at the time was the beautiful steel swing set with 4 board seats attached by heavy-duty chains to the round silver framework. I loved that swing. When I first came to school, I did not know how to "pump" myself into the air, so I would take a run and flop on my belly on that board seat and then lift my legs to have the pleasure of a short swing. I soon learned to pump myself high enough so that the chains would loosen at the very top and the swing would jerk as it began its downward arc.

Our water at the school was provided by using the pump handle at the well to fetch a pail of water for washing and drinking. I have tried to remember, but I have no recollection of ever washing my hands at school. Perhaps there had to have been a wash basin in the entry hall, since it is unlikely it was omitted.

The small toilet building had two rooms. One room had two holes for the boys, but I have no idea what the girls' room looked like. The boys' entrance to the building was on the east and the girls' entrance on the west.

There was a small empty barn behind the school building. Much earlier, when my father's younger siblings were students and my mother was the teacher, it was used to house the horses that the children had ridden to school.

I went to District 37 only one year because my "former teacher" mother did not approve of the way Miss Mathews treated her son. The room was filled with 20 students and as I recall there were 4 of us in grade one. The problem arose due to the fact that my mother during the previous year had the fun of teaching her son at home, everything normally taught in the first grade. I could count, I could read, I could add and no one else in first grade had that ability. I was a nuisance to Miss Mathews---and to the other students. As a precocious bored first grader, I needed something to do, so I whispered. Miss Mathews obviously didn't approve, nor did my less-than-bashful mom who complained of Miss Mathew's solution to the problem. Thus by her prevailing upon the Faribault County School Superintendent at the court house, I was moved to District 97.

The interesting social flavor of this adjustment was that all the kids in District 37 had been of Norwegian descent, while in District 97 everyone was of German descent. I was half and half since my father was Norwegian and my mother was German. So until we attended high school together, I seldom spent time with Duffy except in the summer months.

High school in Blue Earth was a huge adjustment for Duffy and me. We were *"farm"* kids who were seen as having corn cobs hanging out of our ears and having shoes smelling of barn. The societal culture was previously established and we would need to earn our way to belong.

Duffy was two years older than I, so we attended no classes together and he graduated two years previous to me. We only rode the yellow bus together for two years. Yet we became close friends and attended all the high school sports events together.

We each had installed a basketball hoop in the haymow in the barn at our home farm. We spent hours playing "horse" or just being together shooting baskets. While shooting baskets together one day, we jointly planned a "hard-time date". We would double date and take the Blue Earth city girls to a "Frost free show", since these girls had never experienced Frost on Thursday evening in the summer.

Since it was a bit "antique", we used Duffy's father's retired Model-A Ford car for our transportation that evening. The cooling system had a small continuous leak, so Duffy provided a cream can with a supply of water, which stood on the floor between my knees in the back seat.

The girls, Rene and Dotty Factor, agreed in advance to this creative date. On the way to Frost we used only gravel roads and needed to stop once during the six-mile trip to add water.

After sitting on blankets on the lawn to watch the free show, we crossed the street to buy a big watermelon at Issacson's grocery store. Our plan then was to shoot hoops with the girls and eat watermelon the old-fashioned way in the haymow at my home. It was a memorable night. We all had a great time. In spite of the naughty stories sometimes told about girls and boys in the haymow, this was all good fun in a well-lit haymow with a couple of innocent naive farm boys, who shot hoops and ate watermelon slices with two lovely girls, who were really good sports.

During our high school years Duffy and I took turns driving while going on dates, to a movie or to a high school ball game. Anything for an excuse to go to town one evening during the weekend. We often double dated. Rene and I started dating at age 16 as sophomores and she became a constant. Duffy instead enjoyed variety. As a result, Duffy's walking his date to the door took negligible time. As Rene became the only date for me, our relationship became more "comfortable" and we seemingly needed a bit more time to part at the end of each evening. I always appreciated Duffy's seemingly inborn patience.

By the time I reached age 16 I was given the privilege of driving the family 1940 Ford. During the time of WW II gas and many other things including tires were rationed and tires were almost impossible to procure. The rationing board allowed my father to buy a Montgomery Ward trailer which had four new 6.00 x 16 tires. These were quickly exchanged for the worn-out tires from the car. WOW, now we had really good wheels on the car. As the weeks and months of war went on, the tires eventually needed replacement since the rubber quality left a few things to be desired. It seemed during those times we constantly were having flat tires and fixing flats. The rationing board finally allowed Dad to buy two Tri-rib tractor tires for our F-20 Farmall tractor. We really didn't need new tires on the tractor, but we did on the car. We finished the wartime rationing experience with two tractor tires at the front of the family Ford. The Tri-rib tires became terribly bumpy because they wore very unevenly. It was impossible to drive over 30 mph with hexagon-shaped tires.

One evening it was raining hard when it was my turn to drive. I had a flat tire half-way between the Erdahl and the Johnson farms. This was not the first flat that I had experienced, but it was the first that subjected me to pouring rain in the dark. Duffy gracefully said that it wasn't a sensible idea that both of us should get our clothes soaked and *"after all it is 'your' car"*. During that tire-changing ordeal a neighbor came by and loaned a flash light. Soaking wet, my job completed, I continued to the Erdahl farm to deliver Duffy home. Those days were before the time that wearing blue jeans would become acceptable attire to date a girl. We both were wearing good wool slacks. It was still raining hard when we got to Duffy's house. Duffy announced that he did NOT want to get his good well-pressed slacks wet. (Not only did we not wear blue jeans on a date, we both always wore nicely pressed slacks.) So right there in the front seat of the car, Duffy removed his slacks, laid them carefully in the back seat and went into the house, well, just a bit exposed.

After Duffy's father died and Duffy was learning to farm without him, Duffy would approach my father for advice and help. Often my father and Duffy would be repairing something for Duffy in our farm shop. As I write this, I now realize that there was a time that my father's small workshop had more tools than Duffy's shop had. That is astounding, because after my father retired, Duffy's tools and shop have always been one to be admired and among the best in the neighborhood.

My parents and I were not alone in our acceptance and trust of Duffy. Duffy and I often talked about the fact that we seemed like brothers to each other since neither of us actually had a brother. This acceptance and admiration of Duffy continued and was expressed by our intimate family; we insisted that Duffy and his wife, Barbara, sit with us to be included as part of our family at my father's funeral. I knew that Dad would have approved since he and Duffy had enjoyed a portion of the father-son relationship that Duffy lost after his own father's death.

My father was known for his one-liners. I recall one that has resonated with me all my life. He said, *"Victor,* (he never called me Vic) *the most valuable thing you have in this life is your NAME. You can't buy it, you have to earn it."*

I was still quite young, perhaps shortly after Duffy's high school graduation and while I was yet in high school, when Duffy, Rene and I once drove to Prom Ballroom in St. Paul to dance to the music of the big name band called, "Les Bown, The Band of Renown". Duffy had a date with a Blue Earth girl attending Hamline University at the time.

For more than one year, we spent several days attending the state basketball tournaments. I realize now that my parents were very trusting to allow me that much freedom. Part of that trust was because I was with Duffy. My parents loved Duffy and recognized that personal trust in him was obviously well placed. He had earned his good name early in life.

Once when Duffy and I with two other friends went to Minneapolis to attend the state basketball tournament, we stayed at the YMCA for about $3 a night. We learned to enjoy the indoor swimming pool, but it did take a bit of adjustment at first. We learned that it really wasn't bad manners to be required to follow the house rule---No swimming suits allowed. Although we were still naive country boys, we readily adjusted to nude swimming at the YMCA.

I think it was that same trip that we decided to go "raunchy". We had heard about the Alvin Burlesque Theater which was notable for displaying all the attributes dancing girls could possibly display to us country boys----we heard it would be revelations of female bodies like we had never seen before. They undressed and danced to music! I can tell you that now we see more exposure on TV most any evening than what we saw that afternoon at the burlesque show. We could never tell our parents that we had gone to a burlesque show where we saw ladies dance and take their clothes off. Well yes, they almost removed their clothes.

The fondest memory I have of that night happened right after the burlesque show. We were about to walk out the front door when Duffy said, *"Wait a minute."* We all stood back and quizzically watched as he cracked the door open and only allowed his head to stick out, perhaps to see if there was anyone from Dell or Frost out there who might recognize him coming from this sinful place. After surveying the horizon outside, he walked directly to the center of the wide sidewalk, turned an abrupt 90 degrees, and looking straight ahead, began briskly walking and swinging his arms as if he had been just passing by. Obviously he had hoped it would appear to anyone who would happen to see him that he was simply out for an innocent stroll that day. I shook my head in disbelief. It was obvious to us, who followed him out the front door of the theater that day, that Duffy had acquired a serious guilty conscience for attending such a raunchy theater show.

Most every time we went out for a movie or an event or even when we were up in the barn challenging each other to a game of horse or just shooting hoops, Duffy would instigate a theological discussion with me. Anyone that knows Duffy knows that he is a natural-born educator. He sharpened my knowledge of our catechism studies and often challenged my faith, sometimes for hours, while we were shooting baskets, or just sitting on a hay bale, or in the dark in the car after we had returned our dates to their homes.

He could easily recite all of his required catechism memory items. I was impressed that this was so important to him and I enjoyed our lengthy discussions in spite of the fact that the catechism items I had been required to memorize were far less firmly implanted in my memory than were his.

He knew forever the things Pastor Mosby at Dell Church had taught him and he would discuss the Lutheran faith so easily with me, not only because he knew it well, but because of the depth of his faith. I learned much from him since my catechism was in the Evangelical Church located between our farm and Blue Earth. It was a *reformed church* and I soon learned it was reformed from the *Lutheran Church* from which came the basics. I'm sure if one would put all the time that we spent together discussing the faith Pastor Mosby taught him, it would amount to days.

During those serious life-altering discussions, we discussed what we were going to do after we graduated. I was adamant. I was going to be the first name on our family tree that would get a college education. Duffy talked about going to study at LBI, Lutheran Bible Institute. I don't know how long he went there, but I think it may have been for a full school year. I felt that it was important to get college credits He felt compelled to go to LBI even though it offered no college credits. His future wife, Barbara, also attended LBI, but I don't believe they attended at the same time.

During the time that Duffy went to LBI, I went to LaMars, IA to Westmar college. It was a part of our Evangelical Church and my mother was happy that I went to that college. I took classes in pre-engineering.

I tried out for the basketball team, but the coach had been working with his team during the previous summer months so they were a smooth machine. My high school coach was an excellent math teacher, but his coaching skills had not prepared me to easily learn the different set plays that this coach required to play college basketball.

At my high school during the war there remained only two undrafted male teachers from which the superintendant could choose to coach men's sports. I often personally suspected that perhaps Coach Enger may have learned the principles of coaching basketball by briefly studying a really small book.

After one week of college practice with the college team I was dismissed. Of course I can't blame it all on Coach Enger. Those guys were far better equipped to play college ball than a country boy that learned to shoot hoops in the haymow. Thus ended my basketball career.

Next I tried out for college drama. I got a part in a play and had fun. I invited Duffy to come for the production. He came with my parents on the night of the production. Duffy stayed with me several extra days to get a taste of my college life. We had agreed to hitch-hike together the next weekend to return to Blue Earth. We walked to the highway west of town and got our first ride proceeding north for only a few miles. Our next ride took us east with a bib-overalled farmer driving a Model-A Ford pickup who also didn't take us very far. He was a snoose-chewer, who occasionally relieved his "cheekful" against the left side window allowing it to run down inside the door. Duffy and I discovered that the Model-A Ford pick-up cab width had been designed to seat a limit of two people, so to say the three of us enjoyed "a cozy ride" might be a bit overstated.

The next ride was a long time coming. We were now standing patiently somewhere in the middle of the Iowa cornfields, desiring to go either east or north as cars passed by. Finally Duffy said, *"Vic, you're just too big. Nobody wants to take a chance on a big guy like you. Sit down in the ditch and I'll hold my thumb out alone"*

The next vehicle that came was a large gasoline transport. Duffy turned his back and refused to put out his thumb. *"'Why not?* I asked.

Duffy responded, *"A gasoline truck is too dangerous!"*
After the big transport passed, another small truck approached and Duffy was moving his thumb actively. The company logo on the side definitely stood out in large letters, "DUPONT EXPLOSIVES" but this truck, like gasoline transport would not stop for two country boys. Needless to say, I chastised Duffy for attempting to endanger our short lives with a ride that had to be terribly awfully dangerous.

We did make it back to Blue Earth somehow that same day. Those were memorable times when all college people fearlessly hitchhiked quite successfully to go to college and often for pleasure. Life in the Midwest was known to be safely innocent during and for a time following the time of WW II.

I had spent one year studying a pre-engineering course at Westmar College when I transferred to the University of Minnesota. I joined and lived at the Alpha Gamma Rho fraternity located across the street from the U. of M. farm campus. I received a Bachelor of Science degree from the College of Agriculture, Forestry and Home Economics in April 1950, one quarter less than the normal 16 quarters for a degree. My major was Agronomy with a minor in Animal Husbandry.

During my sophomore year at the University of Minnesota, Duffy came to live on the same campus. The "Farm School" utilized the same professors as we had, but only provided high school credits. Unlike the college students who had no dormitory available, the Farm School provided a dormitory for the farm students. Duffy enjoyed the challenge and fun he experienced at the St. Paul U. of M. campus. I teased him mercilessly about the girl friends he chose to squire while there.

Sometime during those early years Duffy felt he was called to be a Lutheran minister. This meant that Duffy would need a long session of college followed by several years of seminary studies. Duffy was persistent. Even at their wedding, the pastor in his homily proclaimed that they would become a marvelous pastor and pastor's wife. I agreed.

Duffy had begun farming after his father's death, but now it was his intention to leave farming to prepare himself for the ministry. He began his search for a farmer with a family who would rent the farm and live on the farmstead. It was a tough sell and he found no one to take the offer. In the meantime Clara, Duffy's Mom, was not agreeing. She was a "stalwart" woman with definite ideas that seldom changed and if she did change, it would take a considerable time, even years to happen. She now declared that she did NOT want Duffy to leave the farm, and that was final. She "needed" him.

Duffy never once told me how he must have agonized deeply when he gave up what he inwardly felt was his calling to be a Lutheran minister. He had to choose between his calling and the biblical requirement to honor his mother. Together, we discussed absolutely everything that might come to the mind of a couple of young virile men as we grew out of adolescence. In all those hours of our discussions, Duffy never spoke negatively about his mother. Clara lived with Barbara and Duffy for the first three years of their marriage; for that reason I remember that my father declared Barbara to be an "Angel".

Duffy had been determined, but quite patient before proposing to Barbara and setting the date. The neighbors and I accused him of being too slow. As I recall, he took seven years. Ragnar Nordaas, one of the neighbors that Duffy enjoyed talking to, told him, *"Duffy, you better get married pretty soon. Women don't like to marry an old man."* Later not to let up on the pressure, Ragnar again chastised Duffy, *"You better get married pretty soon. My wife knows that I always buy her a new dress for every wedding we go to. She really needs a new dress now."*

Duffy, my closest buddy, asked me to be best man at his wedding. I don't think I actually shed tears, but I am sure I felt like it when Duffy stood at the altar and, as his bride walked down the isle, he SANG A SOLO TO HIS BRIDE. Wow, I was really impressed.

He had an ominous feeling on the evening of the wedding, that some of his buddies from Dell were about to pull a naughty trick on him after the wedding, so he advised me thusly, *"Vic, remember your job as best man is to PROTECT me tonight. Remember that you are not just part of the audience, you are MY man!"*

I parked behind Duffy's bullet-shaped 1949 Chevy in front of the church. I watched as his Dell buddies jacked up the right rear wheel and blocked it off the ground with wooden blocks just high enough so the wheel did not quite touch the ground. After the wedding, his buddies were terribly disappointed when just as Duffy started his car, I used my own 49 Chevy to give his a gentle push off the blocks. These were still the days when Chevys had real bumpers.

Rene and I had been dating since our sophomore year in high school. Upon graduating from college, I was 21 years old and we could be married without the necessity of our parents' signature. I knew the law at that time and I had always promised myself that under no circumstances was I going to try to marry before age 21, because it was far beneath my pride to ever beg my mother to allow me to get married. So there!

We were married on June 18, 1950. Duffy was the only person in my acquaintance that ever could qualify for the honor to be the best man at the wedding. He had always been my closest friend.

My first job was as 4-H Agent and Assistant County Agent in the Extension Service of the University of Minnesota. I served with 4 titles in 3 locations in 4 years of employment. I had been 4-H club County director, Assistant County Extension agent, County Extension Agent, and finally Houston County Extension Soils Agent.

In April of 1954 I resigned and returned to Faribault County to begin farming on the farm my grandfather had once owned which was located next door to my parents. I had earned $300 per month during the four years as extension agent, so I had accumulated no savings except an automobile and a used Chevrolet pickup that I had purchased for $300. My father donated 5 purebred Hereford heifers and 3 pregnant sows. I farmed with my father and used his equipment with him until he retired. For the first several years of farming, Rene and I raised chickens to put food on the table. Rene taught school. Money was scarce.

Duffy had been operating his parents' farm almost since graduation from high school. We exchanged labor and tools. We owned a hay baler and a side delivery rake together. We learned how to use farm credit. In fact we had to be frugal since the money from farming was less than either of us expected. For example, Duffy and I each bought a 50 foot electric extension cord and we agreed to share if ever either needed a 100 foot extension cord. I remember asking the farm credit banker for a $300 loan to build a small portable hog house that I would build mostly out of home-sawed cottonwood lumber. The banker refused the additional $300 loan to me.

Duffy and I exchanged labor often whenever either needed an extra hand. Duffy began feeding cattle and I raised hogs and chickens. He did help me castrate little pigs one time. However I never again asked him to help me castrate pigs after the day that he said, *"Ya know Vic, I would rather have cow shit on my face than have pig shit on my shoes!"* Sadly, I understood.

Duffy was known in the neighborhood as the last one to get started planting corn in the spring. But the neighbors were very quiet in the fall because Duffy's corn crop was always the greenest, tallest, and healthiest in the neighborhood and everyone knew that to be true. He was a farmer par-excellent.

I will long remember a conversation I once had with him. I had recently told him that I had been considering the possibility of commuting to St. Paul for four years to get a law degree. I suggested, *"I think we both were destined to always be "quarter-section (160 acres) farmers."*

Duffy answered, *"Not me, Vic."* I was extremely wrong that day; he went on to a much larger farming enterprise. I did not.

I did try my hand at raising cattle like Duffy, only on a smaller scale. Although my father had given me 5 purebred heifers when I first began farming, I soon found that I was not intended to become a purebred Hereford breeder. Each year for three years, I accompanied Duffy on a cattle buying trip to the South St. Paul stockyards to deal with the professional cattle buyers who brought in western cattle for farmers like Duffy and me to buy, feed and eventually sell--hopefully at a profit.

To watch Duffy deal with those professional cattle dealers who negotiated cattle prices every day was a new experience. I was about to see Duffy's patience and persistence in action. Duffy had a way of ignoring time while talking and negotiating until he finally got any expert to lower his asking price far below anything that I had anticipated. I vowed I would never go to buy cattle without Duffy.

I bought 35 head of cattle each of three years that I fed cattle. It was a good investment the first year. I made money. I broke even the second year and I lost money the third year. I quit feeding cattle at that point, but Duffy continued on undeterred. I think he may have been too stubborn to ever admit defeat if he should ever lose and have to feed hogs like me.

I admit that on hot humid days in the summer when the wind was in the south, our outdoor picnic times were impossible due to the hog odor. My Chicago brother-in-law drove into our yard one of those days and as he got out of his car and took one breath exclaimed, *"Phew, that really clears out your tubes!"* We stayed in the house.

Needless to say, through all these years together, we both intimately knew each of the other's faults and strengths. When I became an attorney, I told Duffy that he could always rent my farm and he could set the rent. I knew Duffy would have researched the subject thoroughly and would more than likely pay more than I might have expected. Perhaps it worked that way; however, I've never been sure because our annual rent meeting always took 3 hours and the final amount was negotiated in the last 5 minutes. Each year I could anticipate Duffy's considerate methods of patience and "discussion" trying to prove to me that he actually did not decide the amount of the rent after all. When it was all done, maybe he did and maybe he didn't.

The last story about Duffy's character involves his love of flying. Flying had been a life-long goal of both Duffy and me since we first saw the WW II planes cross the sky above our farms. I remember the day when Duffy and I had our first ride in an airplane on a Sunday sunny summer afternoon early in the 1940 decade. Upon Duffy's urging, we each paid $5 to Art Koskovich to fly with him in a two-place Ercoupe from the Blue Earth airport. On the way home a satisfied Duffy proclaimed with a huge smile, *"I'm going to be a pilot some day!"* I felt the same way, but with my meager assets, I assumed it would be impossible, so I dared not answer Duffy's profound exclamation. In time, like Duffy, I also owned my own personal airplane; I have exceeded my silent hope and lived flying enjoyment beyond my fondest dreams. The evidence of my satisfaction is huge and it has been obvious that the same was true about Duffy's personal joy of flying his airplane.

The sale of his airplane again displays Duffy's gentlemanly way of dealing with all persons. He sold his beloved airplane to a man in the Twin Cities whom he had never before known. This was an emotional day for Duffy. Within a month of the final sale and delivery, the buyer informed Duffy that the engine suddenly needed a serious expensive overhaul that neither Duffy or the buyer had anticipated nor could they have foreseen. What did Duffy do? He offered to pay half of the bill knowing full well he didn't owe it. It was no longer his airplane and he had no obligation of warranty. What did the buyer do? He refused Duffy's offer. That's one time two REAL gentlemen met and did business together. Were all persons like that, there would be far less work for the attorneys.

I know that I am a better person because of the influence of my life-long friend. I expect my sons to follow Duffy's example because everyone in my family admires this man, who had earned and validated his good name by his selfless actions. In my fatherly wisdom, I have admonished my sons that whenever they are dealing with or communicating with another person, they should always ask the question, WHAT WOULD DUFFY DO? One would then have the tools to always protect and earn a most valuable good name just as my father had taught, "***A name can never be bought, it must always be earned.***"

By Vic Johnson
September 2013

Chapter Fifteen

The Story From My Love Life That I Never Told My Wife

When I was a young boy and went to the one-room country schoolhouse called District 97, I had wonderful teachers and received a wonderful education. However the best part of country school was recess time. We had a 15-minute recess in the mid-morning and another in the afternoon, as well as a half-hour recess at noon. We constantly played "kittenball". I found out much later that "town kids" called it softball and it usually was played by GIRLS.

We played "work-up" kittenball. The batter who struck out or got put out while yet on base had to go out to the field and be "last fielder". Then the catcher became batter, the pitcher became catcher and the first baseman became pitcher. That's how you worked up. There were two batters and if there were two batters still on base, well, the one that should have gotten home was OUT. We didn't keep track of the balls, only the strikes since we couldn't pitch that well and we didn't trust anyone who would volunteer to be referee. A game of work-up kittenball would last months because everyone would remember his or her position for the next recess, so that the game could continue to carry on and on.

The thing that impressed me at that time about girls out there in the country school was that girls were awfully clumsy when they tried to catch or throw a ball and were terribly awkward when they tried to bat.

Sometimes we would see a striped gopher pop its head up out of a hole in the school lawn. With only it's head out, as soon as it saw us, it would disappear back into the hole. (Gophers were a nuisance, because of the holes they burrowed under the grass.) We would pump a pail of water to pour into the hole to "drown it out". (The hand-pump over the well was located along the fence on the west side of the playground. All water used in the school was carried in a pail.) The gopher would soon came out running. We would all run after it, to kill it with a ball bat, except the girls, who acted like pansies screaming and holding their hands over their faces. They just weren't with the "program" like the boys were.

When I matriculated to "town school" (Blue Earth High School), I found that no one there played kitten ball. The boys played football and basketball. I had never touched either until I went to town school. The transfer into the 9th grade of town school from district 97 was a tremendous adjustment for this farm kid who only knew how to play kittenball and who knew only that girls were less able players. In my opinion, that was really all I needed to know about girls at that time of my life.

The town kids had already been together in classes for 8 years and country kids were new to the "refined" culture of the town school. As farm kids, we were soon to find out that there was an "in" group and an "out" group socially. Guess what? Farm kids ain't part of the "in-group"! Unrefined country kids that only knew how to play kittenball were obviously not yet accepted socially. It would take a long time for such adjustment to take place. In their opinion the "in-group" looked at us farm kids as having barn manure on our shoes and corn cobs hanging out of our ears. My own adjustment to be accepted into the "in group" would take place only AFTER I became a basketball "jock". This would begin when I was able to play on the second-team in front of the students and the adults from the community. They would all clap and shout when I scored a basket or made an impressive play. (I try to forget the one time that I got confused and shot at the wrong basket. I lived it down after a time because once I was a basketball player, I had become part of the "in-group" so the embarrassment was short-lived.) This wonderful transformation to be accepted by the "in-group" happened in the basketball season of my sophomore year.

What I'm about to describe took place in the fall of my sophomore year, before my wonderful transforming basketball season. Until basketball, my acceptance into the upper society in the class had been completely overlooked by those of the "in group". Before basketball season transpired, I was looked at by the "in crowd" as yet having cornhusks hanging out of my ears which had been somewhat of an improvement over my freshman condition of having the whole ear of corn still exposed.

This was a time that I had heard about some of the guys of the "in-group" who were dating girls in the class. I had never seen any of these town girls try to catch or bat a kittenball, therefore I didn't have a preconceived notion of their lack of athletic status. As a matter of fact, I was beginning to completely overlook the athletic shortcomings that I thought girls normally had, because I hadn't thought of kittenball for a long time. I was beginning to think about more sensitive things. It was true that the town girls now looked pretty good and even began to look attractive. I thought it might be really exciting to date a town girl like the other fellows had done. I wanted to take one to a football game on a Friday night. As I look back, it was obviously a surprising transition time in my life when the red corpuscles and wonderful hormones had began coursing through my veins and arteries to extend to all parts of my body including all my appendages.

My problems were daunting. Which girl shall I ask to go to the football game with me? How do you go about asking a girl to whom you have never had a chance to even talk to? What if she laughs at me? What do you do and how do you act on a date like that? Wow, those are some tremendous problems to surmount.

I watched all the girls in the class for days trying to decide who would be the nicest and who might not laugh at me. Although I knew she was sought after by several of the guys in the class, I decided to try to ask Irene (Rene) to be my date. She was slim, had long blond hair, blue eyes and was really beautiful. All the guys liked her and so did I. There was a big problem. She didn't know I existed. She was in the other section of the class so I had never even heard her talk yet, since we had never spoken to each other.

One day when I was with my parents in the family car, we happened to drive by her house. I had heard that she had 7 brothers and sisters. On that day as we passed by, they were all out in their yard playing a game of family **kittenball**. WOW! Her family could have their own work-up kittenball game. I was doubly impressed. She had to be absolutely special as well as beautiful, although in that short instant while driving by her house that day, I really hadn't seen her bat or catch a ball, so my favorable opinion of her beauty was not biased by her athletic ability or lack thereof. Yes, perhaps I may have felt the first slight pangs of love, but how can I possibly deal with it? It was really scary.

Perhaps I could get a mutual acquaintance to introduce me to her. Naw, that acquaintance would either laugh at me or tell all the other kids about that dumb country boy with corn-husks hanging out of his ears who thinks he could date a lovely gal from the "in-group". I decided it would not be a good idea to involve a third-party since that person would know too much and "spill the beans" for sure. I would have to introduce myself to her or perhaps she could first speak to me some how. It would be easier if she spoke to me first, but that sounded not only unlikely but also seemed impossible at the moment.

Because of my deportment, the principal always had me located near the front of the large study-hall. I had been contemplating how to ask Rene to go to the Friday night football game when she happened to come from her desk far behind mine, and I noticed her slim figure pass me in the aisle next to my desk on my right side. It was noon-hour recess and so this was a time when we were able to talk in the study-hall. I surmised she was going to the restroom. I watched her lithe body stride past my desk on the right side and then turn right at the front of the study-hall. She walked gracefully across the front of the study hall. I kept watching her backside as she disappeared from the study-hall into the darkness of the long hallway. She looked awesome. How could I ever get close enough to her to ask her to go with me to the football game on Friday night? How could I ever get her to talk to me? Hey, there's an idea; **make** her talk to me first. A great idea was developing in my mind.

The desks in the study hall, and all the other rooms for that matter, were too small for my long awkward legs and big feet. For relief, I would slump down in my desk and let my legs rest in the aisle. People using that aisle were sometimes hindered from passing my desk gracefully with those big feet out in the middle of the aisle. Some of the guys would kick my feet to let me know to move them. Some of the girls would just stop in front of my desk and stand silently with their arms folded, until I noticed that I should pull my big feet in and let them pass. Other girls would speak and say, "Would you please let me pass?" I knew instinctively that Rene was one of the wonderful well-bred types who would surely speak to me in that gracious manner when she would come back from the restroom and find my feet blocking her passage. Then I could talk to her after she first spoke to me for the first time in my life. *I now had a plan.*

I hid behind a large encyclopedia, slumped down with the book standing vertical on my desk and put my feet way out in the aisle on the right side where Rene had passed just a minute before so eloquently on her way to the restroom. I ducked behind the book and waited. I peeked out over the corner of the book and saw her as she entered the study hall and begin to walk across the front of the room. I was "very" busy reading, but I could see her over the book as she kept walking. She must have noticed my feet blocking the aisle on the right side of my desk, so to my utter dismay, she went right PAST my row of desks and proceeded to turn toward me to walk by on the LEFT side of my desk. My desk was so close to the front of the study hall that as she was coming down that unprotected side of my desk, there was absolutely no time to study and contemplate a "plan B" before she arrived. She was right beside my desk on the left side and didn't break her stride or even look at me. I had not even seconds to consider the ramifications of the plan B that instantly came to me. I spoke my first words to my beloved to be remembered in eternity. I said,

"Hey, you!"

It may not have been romantic, but she was so surprised that she actually stopped. I stuttered some unremembered words that invited her to go with me to the football game on Friday night. She didn't hear my loud heartbeat nor did she notice the cornhusks still hanging out of my ears. She also left unnoticed the fact that I was not yet a real accepted part of the "in-group". She was graceful, she was eloquent, and she was beautiful. She said, "Sure, I'd like to go with you to the football game on Friday night." I don't recall the rest of the conversation or the rest of the day, because I was too excited and overwhelmed. However, we must have made proper arrangements for a time to meet her at her home on Friday evening before the big game.

I don't remember against which school Blue Earth played that night, nor do I remember the score. I'm just lucky I remembered it was a football game. I doubt that I held her hand or even touched her once, but somehow I must have gotten through that first date without falling on my face, both physically and socially.

We continued to date each other exclusively for our remaining years in high school. I was president of the class our junior year so Rene and I lead the grand march at the junior prom. Rene was president of the class our senior year so Rene and I lead the grand march at the senior prom also. We were accepted by our community as a "couple" and I had long since relieved myself of the "cornhusks hanging from my ears". I was so proud of my choice and that Rene had chosen to join me by my side. She made me feel special and it was all good.

After graduation, Rene began a teacher's training course taught by Miss Drake, whom Rene loved as a teacher. The course was offered as a 5th year class at the high school. In one year of training this would qualify Rene as a teacher in a one-room country schoolhouse, like the one I had enjoyed before coming to "town school".

At the same time, I enrolled in Westmar College at Le Mars, Iowa. Rene and I continued by dating on the weekends when I returned home. One weekend, we began to get serious about our relationship as I began the discussion about the possibility of our marriage. Rene became upset with me. We argued. It was not a good evening. She told me that I could not be so sure she was to be my wife because I hadn't dated any other girls. How could I possibly know if she was the right one, if I hadn't dated other girls for comparison? Maybe I was missing the right person that I should spend my life with because I had not yet dated the right one. I was upset. I was the confident one. It was she that was mixed up, this I knew for sure.

What I didn't know then because of my inexperience was that girls never arrive at decisions of the heart like this in the same way that guys do. Males of the species, Homo Sapiens, use only logic in choosing their mate for life. They are like Alley Oop in the comics, who has a large club shaped like a huge turkey-drumstick over his right shoulder. He has a bearskin hanging from his left shoulder covering his torso to just below his huge knees. In his left hand he has the thick black hair of his "chosen" as he drags her into his cave. He has used *logic* as the sole consideration in the choice of his mate.

The female of the species, Homo Sapiens, hardly uses logic at all when she chooses a mate. Instead she uses feelings and emotions. She displays these feelings and emotions only partially and when she does they are called "nuances". These feelings and nuances to the male are like a "red fishing-bobber" floating on the lake. Depending on the condition of the lake, the red fishing-bobber can go up and down with the change of other outside influences, like wind and weather. If the weather becomes really stormy, the red fishing-bobber can even go out of sight. God, in his genius, did not equip the male of the species, Homo Sapiens, to be able to understand these feelings and emotions, nor can the male read the nuances correctly as they change unannounced from time to time like a red fishing-bobber. The poor male has been only equipped with his logic to try to understand the puzzle, so he is hopelessly confused. Somehow God must have intended it to be this way, because this has been a truth since time began and continues to this day.

The male of the species, Homo Sapiens, by design, has always been ill-equipped to understand the female's feelings, as her nuances go right past him without being interpreted. His only defense is his logic and it is never adequate for this delicate job of interpreting female nuances.

Being all of 18 years of age, I was no better than Alley Oop. The waters on "our lake" seemed all riled at this stormy time in my life. Now the red fishing-bobber was completely removed from sight. She had told me that she really didn't want me, because she knew that I really didn't know what I wanted. I had unsuccessfully argued against her conclusion and lost. She said that we would no longer be "going together". Oh, we had temporarily broken up before, but this was the first time that the red fishing-bobber had completely disappeared from sight. Yet I chose to be persistent enough not to give up without trying to somehow attempt to change her mind. I was quite sure that if I would treat her just right and say just the right words, perhaps time would heal some of the rough water on "our lake". I was actually hoping that the " blue water on our lake" next weekend would be smooth and quiet, when I would come to see her, so that the red fishing-bobber would come back into sight and not bounce all over the water.

I lucked out. On Sunday, the next day after our breakup, my father said that he needed me to help him the following weekend with the spring fieldwork on our farm. He suggested that I take the 1940 Ford family car to college for the next week and return promptly on the following Friday evening for me to be able to help with the field-work on Saturday and Sunday.

For a whole week I would have wheels! This was right after World War II and there was only one other guy on campus with a car. Surely now equipped with a car, I could easily entice a lovely co-ed to go on a date with me sometime during that week. Then I would be able to show Rene that I was experienced and know what I really wanted, if we discussed marriage the following weekend. Good deal! I was excited about my wonderful new adventure and plan.

I was obviously still too inexperienced to be able to foresee the disaster awaiting me. I had not considered the dire consequences of this plan. Imagine that I would have a wonderful date with a gorgeous, beautiful, elegant co-ed. Then I would come back to Blue Earth to tell Rene all about the wonderful date which would now qualify me to be acceptable to her. Really?

I had completely overlooked this possible disaster in the making. I had not thought about it, but there would be two possible scenarios that could happen, if I announced to Rene that I actually had this wonderful successful date with this gorgeous, beautiful, elegant co-ed. One possibility would be that I would find myself out cold on the floor. That possibility was really unlikely since Rene had never previously exhibited violence. So the more likely scenario would be that I would find myself left all alone in the room. She would have left without a comment of any sort. And there sits "Alley Oop" all alone and totally confused. I didn't know it at the time, but my wonderful logic was seriously flawed before the week even began to unfold.

That week on campus was similar to the time when I was a high school sophomore and pondered my first date with Rene. Once again, I contemplated which co-ed would be the one to invite on a date. I chose one lovely lass that previously had been steadily dating but I had heard that they had broken up and had called it off. I approached her in the dining hall on Tuesday and asked her as follows, *"How would you like to go with me to Orange City on Thursday night after classes at 4 pm, to see the tulip festival? I hear it's really nice and fortunately I have a car this week. How about it?"* After she accepted graciously, I said, *"There is a rear seat in the car, which obviously would be room for another couple. Why don't you ask one of your friends who has a date to go along with us?"*

The girls at the college were all housed in the girls dormitory and in my opinion, they all seemed to treat each other like sisters. The guys didn't have a dormitory and were housed in private homes all over town. She said, *"Well, who do you want to go with us?"*

I said, *"I don't really know your friends, so I will leave it up to you to bring anther couple."* It was agreed and I was looking forward to my big date to prove my manliness to Rene. I would now be able to tell Rene that I was an experienced guy who had dated another girl. Unbeknownst to me I was headed toward certain disaster the next weekend.

Promptly at 4 pm, I drove our 1940 Ford green sedan to the girls' dormitory. First to come out were Willis Goettel and his date. I had seen them together often in the past and I was relieved to think we would have Willis and his date along with us in the rear seat. Right behind Willis and his date was another co-ed, who happened to be my date's roommate. To my surprise, she proceeded to get into the passenger seat of the Ford, seating herself right beside me. I was totally perplexed. I said, *"Where is _____?"* (I have long since forgotten my intended date's name.)

The roommate answered, *"Oh, she sent me instead."* I was flabbergasted. I was speechless. I was becoming angry. My knees grew weakened. My ego hit a new low.

It was suddenly obvious that I was totally unable to actually get an actual date with a lovely co-ed. I had been "stood up". I would never be able to tell Rene that I had a lovely date with a co-ed at college. I would not be able to convince her that I really did know who I wanted as a life mate, when I told her that she was my choice of a soulmate. This had been my only chance and I had failed; really, I had failed badly. My manliness was on the line and I was a total disaster.

There were few words uttered by the couple in the front seat of the 1940 Ford either going or returning from the tulip festival at Orange City, Iowa, that day. I was so angry and my spirits so low that I could hardly turn my head to look in the direction of my date's roommate sitting by my side. I have no idea how the tulips looked in Orange City, and I have no actual recollection of even seeing any tulips. Willis and his date in the rear seat perhaps had a great time, for all I know, because I was too busy licking my wounds to notice.

When we returned to the girls' dormitory, I reached across to open the passenger door for her and perhaps said something innocuous as she got out. I didn't leave my seat from behind the wheel of the Ford. I was not a proper gentleman. That afternoon I had not so much as touched her hand. I had been **"HAD" royally.** I miserably failed to prove my manliness with my preplanned event.

Two of my intended date's girl friends came to me the next morning on the way to classes to tell me that they had scolded my proposed date. They had let her know that it was a mean dastardly trick that she had played on me and she must apologize to me.

That noon she did come to me and said, *"Vic, I'm really sorry for what I did to you yesterday. I know what I did was wrong and I'm sorry. I will go with you anytime that you would ask me. Please forgive me."*

I have no idea what my response was, but I was thinking, "You blew your only chance, Babe. See ya. I've got a much better deal back in Blue Earth, I hope. And since it's Friday, I'm really not available, because I'll be driving to Blue Earth this afternoon."

Though no fault of my own, fate had actually protected me and had intervened upon my careful plan which had been built entirely on logic. Fate had saved me from utter disaster. Rene would never hear of my failure to prove myself to her in the manner I had planned. She would never hear the failed story from my past. I could never tell her. It was too painful. It should have been a life-changing event of conquest, that I thought I needed to prove my manliness.

On Friday night I returned the 1940 Ford to my father. I did see Rene on Saturday night. Fortunately on that night, the water on "our lake"was calm and the "red fishing bobber" just floated quietly and pleasantly, as my remaining attributes proved to be acceptable by my chosen one.

On that night, for some unknown reason, I really didn't need to prove that I had a date with some co-ed to be accepted by Rene. The nuances that usually flew right over my head, must have been abated and pacified somehow on that eventful night. Just like Alley Oop, I hadn't been able to read the nuances effectively and still couldn't. Yet on that eventful evening I was successful even though I had used my only "tool" to choose Rene as my life long soulmate. The only tool I had was *logic*.

As I continued to love my chosen and receive her love, the positive feelings and emotions that I received from her could never be classified as a "tool", but rather it was a fabulous rich reward that I received and accumulated over the many years ahead. Even so, that reward seemed to never include an ability to read nuances. God did not intend man to have that gift, remember?

We waited until I finished college to be married in June of 1950. At that time, apparently adulthood commenced only when one reached the age of 21, because had we chosen to marry before reaching that age, we would have needed our parents' signed consent on the marriage application. There was no way I would ever ask my loving, but controlling and domineering, mother to sign our marriage application. This was a decision that I would make as an adult without involving parents. We had paid our dues with the growing pains of young love and now we could become soulmates by our own adult choice.

The rest of the story is that we lived happily ever after for 54 years. But those of you who are married know that there is an important and true caveat to that simple statement. Actually it properly should be said that we lived happily ever after, ***most of the time.***

Vic Johnson
October 21, 2004

Our wedding, June 18, 1950.

Chapter Sixteen

Eulogy

Irene Lucille Christianson Johnson
Born March 12, 1928 - Died June 6, 2004

W hen I think of my soul mate of almost 54 years, whether I start at the beginning of the moving picture of her life and fast forward or whether I start at the end of the moving picture of her life and fast reverse, every picture seems to include children. She super-loved her daughter, her sons and her grandchildren; she couldn't pass a baby in the arms of a mother on the street or in church without loving the child; nor could she pass a child being pushed in a baby stroller without talking to and touching the child, even though that child's mother was a perfect stranger. Although we needed the money at the times she taught kindergarten, I believe she would have taught without payment if she were asked. I had to trust Superintendent Ken Queensland not to ask.

As I thought of her in my mind's eye with a group of children, I couldn't help but think of a song about another woman from the movie and drama, "The Sound of Music," who also loved to be with children. Although Maria is a different name than Rene or Irene, yet now when I hear words to the song about Maria, I can only think of Rene instead of Maria. The words go like this:

> *How do you solve a problem like Maria?*
> *How do you catch a cloud and pin it down?*
> *How do you find a word that means Maria?*
> *Many a thing I'd like to tell her.*
> *Many a thing she ought to understand.*
> *But how do you make her stay*
> *And listen to all I have to say?*
> *How do you keep a wave upon the sand?*
> *How do you solve a problem like Maria?*
> *How do you catch a moonbeam in your hand?*

Rene always displayed the same child's heart that was so eloquently portrayed in the character, Maria, in the song and the story. Rene has always loved to be in the presence of children and react with them and react like them. Jesus said, *"Let the little children come unto me."* So I have to believe that has included Rene since she kept her child's heart even to the end of her time and even after many other loving attributes seemed to have been deleted from her memory.

God had given me the responsibility of caring for a most precious gift 54 years ago when I committed to the covenant of marriage involving the loveliest human being I had ever met. At that time and ever since, she has had grace, elegance, a Christian compassion, and a beautiful spirit. I have always been proud to have her by my side throughout our marriage because she had her own colorful way, often purple or teal, to display that grace and elegance. She unceasingly shared her beautiful Christian compassion with everyone that she met by freely giving positive compliments to stranger or friend. By her loving actions she even made me look good.

Was it always a beautiful, a perfect marriage and did she also always share positive compliments to me at all times? Now I could fib and say, *"Yes."* However, we learned very early on, that marital love just doesn't happen by itself. Like a flower garden, it has to always be cultivated. Sometimes in the past Rene and I had some really big weeds to pull out. One time when Mrs. Billy Graham was asked if she had ever considered divorce during their long marriage, she answered, *"Never divorce, but sometimes murder!"* Obviously Mrs. Graham and I have long since learned to cultivate.

Rene and I have struggled with the disease of Alzheimer's for nine years, me as her caregiver and she as the victim of that dread disease. As we recently read of President Reagan's plight, we have learned that the disease is referred to as the "slow goodbye." Over time, as Rene changed and as the disease took its ugly toll, Rene always found security in two places: her home and me being in her presence. We automatically held hands whenever we were not in our home. We both liked that. When I would be gone for even a few minutes when we were not at our home, she would ask,

"Where is Vic?"

As I found myself gradually being immersed into the full-time profession of being a caregiver to my chosen, who now was afflicted with dementia, I needed to change some of my own learned attributes. Fortunately study and research showed that there were only two very simple basic rules that I must follow to succeed as a caregiver to Rene

Rule #1. I had to realize and always at all times remember that after Rene was afflicted, the first thing that was lost from her memory is what is colloquially referred at her "reasoner". This would never again be available to Rene. I had to understand that Rene was now forever unable to learn anything new nor could I ever correct her by logical reasoning.

Rule #2. This rule was simpler for me to understand. I could never, never raise my voice in frustration because I must ever be patient with love, love, love and then some more love to Rene for the rest of our days together. I now needed to prove my love to her by at all times following these two rules for our sake even when I was tempted otherwise.

Several weeks ago, I arose early before Rene awakened on a Sunday morning. I read some things that other caregivers had written and then my writing juices started to flow, although I didn't originally have any intention of writing anything. This is what I wrote before we went to church on that day.

It was Christmas 1996 that Rene did not prepare any gifts for the children and grandchildren, as had been her usual loving custom. We were to have our traditional family gathering at the home of my son and his family in Minneapolis. This change was because on this Christmas we no longer had a house due to our devastating house fire that previous July. Just hours before we arrived, realizing we had no gifts yet, we had purchased some token gifts to give to each family. When we gave our gifts to our children, Rene asked, *"Who gave those gifts?"* That was when first I realized that something drastic and terrible had happened. The meaning of dementia struck home as never before, like a dense stone sinking to the bottom of my gut. It will never be recovered, never be returned to its rightful place on some unexplored shelf of unthinkable abominations.

In January 2001 the second shoe dropped. It was not the small strokes that the experts had observed on her MRI taken in 1998 that caused her dementia; it now was "probable Alzheimer's disease." We learned that all that Rene was, all she is or ever will be, is now given to our own memory, and in the future, to what we were to observe about her, day by excruciating day. What can we remember? What memory can we carry forward and keep so that it does not fly off somewhere like bodies from the centrifugal wheel at the playground? There must be some recollections at the very center that we can bring to mind and say, *"That was her!"* or *"Let me tell you what she was like!"* Something that remains, that is denser than the densest stone, yet light enough to pass on down through the generation without ever falling to the ground.

Vic Johnson - May 16, 2004
(Composed 21 days before her death)

At the time I wrote that piece titled "Memory," Alzheimer's disease had changed the presence of Rene and according to all accounts was going to do more ugly devastation, as time would go on. After she would leave me in death, I wanted to remember and I wanted every one else first and foremost to remember the Rene that was like Maria in the song and not the Rene that had been hollowed out by a terrible disease. I needn't have been concerned. In my mind now she remains that loveliest human being that I first fell in love with and to whom I made that covenant of marriage. Yes, the memory of her that the loving hand of God has caused to be retained is her healthy colorful image dressed in purple and teal and that memory truly is indelible.

Today as I rerun that moving picture in my mind's eye of my life together with Rene for 54 years, I remember that we have had a wonderful joy-filled life together, that we have overcome many adversities and relished so many rainbows. I think the prophet Isaiah had it right on target when he advised us long ago as follows:

He gives the power to the faint,
And strengthens the powerless.
Even youths will faint and be weary,
And the young will fall exhausted;
But those who wait for the Lord
will renew their strength,
They shall mount up with wings like eagles,
they shall walk and not faint.

God's grace is sufficient. God is good. Praise be to God.

Epilogue

WHAT EACH GENERATION WAS DOING AT AGE 25

After all the stories here were completed, my son, Dana, suggested that since Ole Iverson staked out his homestead claim and built the sod house at age 25, perhaps it might be interesting to compare what the men in each generation thereafter were doing at age 25.

Skaffar-Ivar, born 1807. 25 years later—1832

According to the records, both Skaffar-Ivar and his father were Skaffars, (transportation-for-hire) so it can be assumed that at age 25, he too was involved in that occupation.

Ole Iverson, born 1835. 25 years later—1860

It has been assumed that Ole staked-out his homestead in 1860, but it could have been during the span of 1860-1863, However, Ole could also have been preparing to travel or traveling to Faribault County, Minnesota during those three years.

Ole Johnson, born 1869. 25 years later—1894

Ole Johnson was married in 1893 and bought his farm in 1894, a portion of the original homestead area.

Joseph Johnson, born 1895. 25 years later—1920

Joseph served in the Navy in WWI from 1918 to 1921. He was on board the ship 'De Kalb' which formerly was a German ship which had been captured. They were at sea for 5 days, but two days before arriving at Nice, France, the Armistice was signed on November 11, 1918 ending the war. They delivered 6000 mail bags to Nice, France and returned with the ship overloaded with returning servicemen. Joseph returned home in 1919, but was in the Naval Reserves until 1921. Perhaps he may have started farming in 1920. He married Elsie Alma Fenske in 1921 and lived in the Iverson white house upon marriage and thereafter until retirement.

Victor Johnson, born 1928. 25 years later—1953

Victor (the author) graduated from the University of Minnesota in April of 1950. After graduation, he was employed as an instructor and County Extension Agent in southern Minnesota until April 1954 when he resigned and moved to the Ole Johnson farmstead in Faribault County, Minnesota to begin farming. At that time he already had a daughter, Pamela, born in 1952. Dana was "on the way" being born on August 2, 1954

Dana Johnson born 1954. 25 years later—1979

Dana married Phoebe Steneman on June 17, 1978 and began his long-time employment with Fastenal, Inc. that year, which will continue until his retirement.

Seth Johnson and Adam Johnson,
Identical twins, born 1983. 25 years later—2008

These brothers joke that they subscribed to the 4 to 8 year college program without the necessity of a Ph.D. Actually, both of them were working in 2008, while with part-time attendance, they completed their credit requirements for their degrees.

Addendum 1

John W. Iverson

Ole's brother, John Iverson Vikoren, was 11 years old in 1856, when they immigrated to America. Eight persons named (from) Vikoren (later Vik or Vig) went together on that trip, so John and Ole were part of a group. Karl Ingebriktsen Vikoren was another 11 year-old boy that traveled to the U.S. without parents, so John had a friend that was his age on that voyage.

Their brother, Johannes, who was two years younger than John, immigrated five years after Ole and John had left Norway. One time Johannes and some comrades went to a dance hall in the U.S. At the entrance was a doorman who argued and denied them entrance. Johannes, intending to enter, took the doorman's arm and, pushing him aside, said, *"You will be hit by one of Norwegian blood!"*

The doorman began to reply, *"You will be hit by one with Norwegian blood, too"*; but he stopped and asked, *"Where are you from?"*

Johannes answered, *"I am from Vik in Sogn, I"*.

John, who was the doorman that night, replied, *"I am, too. Whose son are you?"*

"Skaffar-Ivar, I", said Johannes.

The two brothers, who had not seen each other since childhood, now met as adults. With mixed emotions, tears flowed and neither of them entered the dance hall that night after their surprise reunion.

John joined the military for four years, serving in the 9th Iowa Regiment during the Civil War, taking part in more than 40 battles.

I found limited information that provided that he married Marget and had their first child in 1869.

John served as a conductor for the Chicago & Northwestern Railway from 1886, first in Chicago, and later in Yankton, S.D. where at his death in 1912, he held the record as the oldest conductor in service for that railroad. He was buried in Boone Co. Illinois, where many had settled upon immigration from Vik.

Addendum 2

Guttorm Tistel

Letter written by Guttorm Tistel, brother of Endre (Andrew), which he sent back to Norway after arriving and settling down in the USA at Boone County, Illinois.

This letter was translated by Viggo Fosse from Norway for Diane Jones. Viggo does not think there are any actual copies of the letter available anywhere.

Caption in the Yearbook (Old letter in Drammen Tiden): "Letter from Guttorm Tistel (1808-1885) dated 1844. He emigrated in 1843 with his wife Brita Ellingsdatter Føli (1821-1843) and their daughter Torbjørg. This letter was published in the newspaper "*Tiden*" in Drammen on May 29, 1844. The letter gives a realistic and detailed picture of the strenuous journey across the Atlantic, and towards their destination in America. Guttorm lost his wife and daughter on this journey, and several others in their party succumbed. In the letter he also gives a vivid description of life in America."

Chicago January 3, 1844

Greetings to friends and relatives!

Initially I will advise anyone who intends to travel to America that they establish a contract with the Captain with whom they intend to emigrate. The least amount of water you must bring onboard is

3 "potter" (=3 pots) per day, but we did not get more than 2 "pægle" and we were therefore ready to die of thirst. Neither was it of good quality, and it had such a bad taste and foul smelling that we had to vomit.

When departing from Bergen you do not run a risk if you exchange 5 "francs, piastre, dubloner, Norske sølvspecier", but not any small change. When you arrive in New York be careful not to exchange any gold coins as there are lots of false ones around made of tin and glass. Here too you are requested to establish a contract with the Captain who offers to bring you up the canals. Several will present themselves to do the job, but you have to be careful. You are requested not to sail on freighters, but rather on steamers who arrive at their destination 14 days ahead of the freighters. It costs only 2 dollars more. I and my company traveled on a freighter and spent more than a month on board, and we had a hard time. There were no place to sit or stand, and we were stowed away like pigs. While traveling up the canal we had such good weather we could walk on the shore along the canal. During the trip we collected so much fruit, especially apples, which we brought onboard the ship in big sacks. Be careful not to eat too much of this fruit as you acquire various diseases.

I will also let you know a little about the nature of the land, and how my life is. When I arrived here I undertook a journey of 130 mile up the country. Another man and I were hired by a gentleman in Chicago, and we were paid 5 dollars each to bring back 3 cows and 2 heifers. We were in the area where Peder Undi of Vik and Sand Ulum (=Sjur Ulvund) and Peder Skjærvum (=Skjervheim) from Voss were residing. They were all well off and were living like "storfold" (=well situated people). Peder Skjærvum had 50 pigs who were grazing in the woods, and were herded home only a few times per week to be marked. These pigs who feed themselves are so fat, and there's nothing like it in Norway. There are homesteaders here who have 250 to 500 pigs. The grass is so tall you have to protect your face and eyes when you walk in the pastures, and the fields with Indian corn are enormous. The Indian corn looks like peas and there are about 1000n seeds per cob. From each acre they can harvest 15 to 20 barrels of wheat, and they do not have to fertilize the fields. You will find it peculiar that no man has more than one house. There are no houses for the cattle or pigs as they are feeding themselves in the thick forests during summer as well as during the winter. Normally a farm labourer cuts enough grass for one cow per day. The grass is stored in large haystacks and during winter they cut the feed from these in appropriate portions, just like cutting a cheese. You are not requested to bring any work tools. Here you will find the necessary tools, and the prices are low. The price of butter is 10 cents per pound, bacon is 3 cents, meat 1 cent, wheat 1 cent and for 1 barrel of pig feed it is 25 cents. You would never have seen such large amounts of slaughtered pigs. Often you will observe more than 1000 laid on wooden tables. Theft is a very rare event here, and the Law and Church customs are good.

I will now have to think on finishing this letter, but I will have to report who has passed away in our company. The last night we stayed in Buffalo (on Sept 22) my wife was taken ill, but we had to travel an additional 500 miles. When we arrived in Chicago on Sept 29 she died on the journey at 4 o'clock in the morning. She was buried at 7 o'clock the same morning. Then my daughter Torjørg was taken ill. I was taken by grief and exhaustion, and 8 days later she died. I brought her to our destination where she was laid to rest. Anna Gulteigen died on the journey, as well. On Oct 9 we arrived at a place in Chicago where we intended to settle. At that time Erik Undi and Guldteigen from Vik were taken ill. They were buried the same day their brother, who had been here 2 years, came to welcome them. Ole Guldheigen died too. Hans from Dalen was taken ill as well and at about Thanksgiving time he had to be transported on a wagon up the country. It was so cold for 9 days that you were unable to keep warm by walking. A few days before they arrived at their destination Hans passed away.

As you will know, I did not have sufficient money to buy land. Therefore I purchased a fully equipped small house with 3 rooms, and an oven/stove for 65 "specidollers". I live in this house, and I have 3 Norwegian families as lodgers and for this I get paid 2 "speciedoller" and 12 "shilling" per week. When I get to have the house expanded somewhat I think I could make a living of it.

Finally, I will let you know that I do not recommend anyone with children to undertake the journey across the ocean to America. The travel is exceedingly strenuous, and rarely without outbreak of diseases and misery. Unmarried people ("løse folk") may travel through. They have none to care about, and here's room and work for all. I will now end my letter with sincere greetings.

Guttorm Tistel

About the Author

Victor Johnson was born and raised on one of the two building sites located on the original Iverson homestead in Faribault County, near Blue Earth, Minnesota. He, his sister Evelyn, and his parents Joseph and Elsie Johnson lived in the original frame house built by homesteader, Ole Iverson. This house had been preceded by the sod house and the log cabin. During the author's childhood, his grandparents, Ole and Martha Johnson lived next door about a quarter-mile away.

He began his elementary education in a one-room country school located about a mile from his home. He graduated from Blue Earth High School in 1946 and received a Bachelor of Science degree from the University of Minnesota College of Agriculture, Forestry and Home Economics in April, 1950. After graduation, for 4 years he was an instructor for the University of Minnesota as an Agricultural Extension Agent in southern Minnesota.

He married Irene Christianson Johnson in 1950 and they had four children, Pamela Renee, Dana Jerome, Matthew Conrad and Jayson Christian.

The young couple returned to the homestead in 1954 and purchased his grandfather Ole Johnson's farm. For 17 annual crops, he was a farmer, raising corn, soybeans, flax and various farm livestock.

During these years, Irene (Rene) taught school at Delavan and at Blue Earth. She had completed her bachelor's degree and the class credit requirements for her master's degree at Mankato State Teachers college. Then one day, she suggested to her husband that he might like to take some additional college credits. At that time money was scarce and the family size was increasing.

Victor tells the story that he accepted his wife's challenge because, he said that, *"We should begin to pay some taxes to the IRS"*.

At age 36, he began night law school at William Mitchell College of Law in St. Paul, MN, by commuting from the farm to St. Paul for four years to get his Juris Doctor degree. It took 25,000 miles (or about the same distance as around the world at the equator) for him to become a lawyer, as he contined working his farming operation; he used his "spare time" working as a legal assistant for the Blue Earth law firm while attending law school.

The law firm with which he partnered upon graduation, was known as Putnam, Spencer and Johnson. After the death of the senior partner, the firm became Spencer, Johnson and Richards.

The question is often asked by anyone outside of the rural farm area in southern Minnesota, "What type of law do you practice?" He always answered, *"We were experts at whatever was presented when the farmer or business person walked in the front door of our office"*.

During their 17 farming years, Victor and Irene spent many evenings with house plans, magazines and a drawing board, because the couple had no TV and had dreamed of building a new home to replace the house that Ole Johnson had built. They designed a 5-bedroom 'Dutch Colonial home', built in 1966 (much of it done with Victor's carpentry skills) to accommodate their family, which included Irene's mother, Grandma Ann Christianson.

Irene was diagnosed with Alzheimer's disease in 1996 and began the "nine-year slow death." That same year a house fire destroyed their home, just two years after Victor's retirement from his law practice. The damaged house was completely cleared out, except the remaining bare boards, to begin the rebuilding. With the help of two carpenters for three weeks, and the help of neighbors and family, Victor became a finish carpenter again and rebuilt their home, which was larger than necessary for just two occupants.

Alzheimer's took its final toll on Irene, who died in 2004. During these nine years, her husband cared for her 24/7 at home, while patiently continuing the rebuilding of their home.

A year later, Victor met and married Eleanor Lindeman and they lived together on the farm for six years, until moving to Inver Grove Heights, MN in 2012.

The two building sites on the original homestead (but not the agricultural land) were sold in 2012 and for the first time since 1861, a portion of the original homestead would be owned by persons not in the Iverson family lineage.

These stories of "Life Since the Iverson Sod House" for the past 156 years will continue endlessly into the future and will be told by others who come after the lives that were told of here; they shall continue this unfinished story that began with a simple house made with bricks of prairie sod.